How to feed your toddler

How to feed your toddler

Everything you need
to know to raise happy,
independent little eaters

CHARLOTTE STIRLING-REED

CONTENTS

INTRODUCTION

The weaning stage can be tough, with lots of uncertainties, and that's why I loved writing *How to Wean Your Baby*. However, often the uncertainties with feeding don't just stop when your baby reaches 12 months and, when it comes to the toddler years, parents often wonder 'What happens next?' That's exactly where this book comes in...

How to Feed Your Toddler is all about the next steps on your feeding journey – starting at 12 months, right through to preschool age – and aims to make this next hurdle fun and fill you with confidence! This book takes the science and evidence on toddler nutrition and breaks it down into digestible, easy-to-understand messages for tired, time-poor parents/carers like myself.

Parental confidence can be key when it comes to knowing what to do about feeding kids. Most of us are somewhat winging it along our parenting journey and you might feel the same when it comes to feeding your little one. This is completely normal and if you're thinking a lot about how to feed your toddler, you're probably already doing much better than you think.

How to Feed Your Toddler aims to take the stress out of toddler mealtimes, stop any feelings of guilt and make the whole experience much more enjoyable. I'm not saying that there won't be ups and downs, but hopefully after reading this book you'll feel more equipped to deal with those little bumps along the way and be more confident about *how* to feed your toddler. There is never one single approach to feeding children that works for all; it might take a bit of trial and error, and sometimes you need to find out what works best for you and your family. Also, how your toddler has progressed so far with their food journey is likely to vary from family to family, so everyone will have different starting points. Sometimes just knowing that there will be bumps in the road when it comes to children's eating can help to reassure us and take the pressure off. I find remembering that 'it's just a phase' on a regular basis helps.

Feeding toddlers can be a time of nurturing, engagement and even some hilarious moments, which we can enjoy all the more if we feel relaxed and confident about how to feed them.

WHAT TO EXPECT

In this book you'll learn how to:

- Cope with the dreaded fussy eating phase and create happy mealtimes
- Balance your toddler's diet and get inspiration for meals
- Navigate eating out of the home, including at nursery

All of this has been written with the current guidelines on feeding toddlers in mind, drawing on expert guidance and my own experience. I've also included a delicious recipe section, offering 50 recipes that are suitable for the whole family, as well as a handy troubleshooting section. Ultimately, my hope is that this fully comprehensive book will help you raise children who really love their food.

Note: Throughout this book I've used parents/carers interchangeably to refer to anyone who is caring for a little one!

SOME REASSURANCE BEFORE WE BEGIN

The early years are a great time to be thinking about your toddler's diet – they are growing so quickly and the food they eat will be laying down the foundations to help them in their future health too. So getting them used to and familiar with a healthy, well-balanced diet may mean they are also more likely to eat well as they get older. Patterns of eating and food behaviours are developed when our kids are young, so if you want to help your child explore and enjoy a wide variety of foods, you've come to the right place!

Additionally, children are incredibly resilient, and even during periods of picky eating where they are selective about their foods, growth and nutrition are not likely to take much of a hit in the long run. Periods of food refusal are part of the journey and this book will show you how to navigate all of this.

A BIT ABOUT ME

Having two children myself, I am currently on the journey of feeding toddlers. My daughter, Adaline, is now two and my son, Raffy, has just turned five, and feeding both of them has really helped to shape and inform the advice I give out to parents. It's not as easy as simply 'Follow these guidelines and all will be well'. Additionally, with all the will in the world, sometimes the standard advice just doesn't cut it and parents need more support and more detail. Children are also a minefield in themselves – there are so many yo-yos of emotions within a given few minutes, let alone days, weeks and years. We've been through the lot and have seen multiple periods of food fussiness, especially with my son Raffy.

My practical, in-depth, hands-on experience with my two has really helped me see the ultimate dos and don'ts of feeding toddlers; what works and what really doesn't when it comes to getting them to eat and enjoy their foods. This, combined with tons of research into this area, working in this field for many years and speaking to thousands of parents on a regular basis, has helped me to write it all down here in my very own guide!

My 5 key principles

When it comes to feeding both babies and toddlers, I think it is important to step back from the idea of 'getting your child to eat' and instead have a look at the atmosphere at mealtimes. There are a few key principles that can support your little one to eat well, and help if you find that your toddler is going through a fussy patch. These are the cornerstones that I believe can really help to establish happy, healthy little eaters.

1. Eat together: role model where possible

Often children model themselves on their parents and copy their choices, eating behaviours and attitudes towards food. If children grow up seeing food as an important part of family life and as something to be enjoyed, rather than a necessity, it's likely that they will learn to be little foodies themselves and hopefully love a variety of foods. *Show* your toddler what and how to eat as well as how to enjoy foods and mealtimes. This includes demonstrating how to eat a balanced diet – if you show your child that you enjoy variety and like plenty of balance, they are more likely to follow in your footsteps. This doesn't mean you have to sit with your toddler and always eat the same foods as them. However, you can try to make the most of mealtimes together as and when you can – perhaps at the weekend – or aim for someone from the family to have one meal with them most days.

2. Avoid pressuring to eat

So much research shows that pressuring little ones to eat is likely to backfire. When we put pressure on children to eat, or to eat certain foods, the food we're pressuring them to eat becomes less desirable, mealtimes become less enjoyable and their relationship with foods/eating/mealtimes is likely to take a hit. Even a little coaxing such as 'Just one more spoon', 'Please eat it – I just spent 40 minutes making that' or 'We don't waste food in this house' can have this effect too. Mealtime pressure stops children listening to their own appetites and encourages them to ignore their body's signals of fullness.

3. Listen to your child and get them involved

Listen to your little one and let them play a big part in their own journey around food. For example, if they say they're full and don't want any more, respect that. If they say they don't want broccoli today, respect that too.

In addition, your responses as a parent are so key, so if your child tells you 'I'm not hungry' (even if they are) and you respond by saying 'That's OK, you don't have to eat it if you're full' and you do this consistently, they'll likely learn that they won't be forced to eat and that they are in charge of their own appetite. Giving them a choice at mealtimes can help too. Simply asking, 'Would you like peas or carrots with dinner tonight?' helps them to feel more involved in what's on offer.

Stepping back from mealtimes and getting kids involved in meal prep, shopping, gardening, cooking and involving them in play around food can all help make foods more fun and familiar.

4. Keep trying with foods

Children's appetites are often fickle and ever-changing, so just because they say they don't like a meal you've made or a food you're offering, it doesn't mean they won't learn to like it later. The key thing here is *familiarity*. Kids like what they know. So if your toddler tells you one day that they don't like broccoli, you can respect that and allow them to leave it on their plates without striking it off the menu going forward. Keep offering a variety, even the refused options, and in the long run they are likely to accept these again at some point.

In doing so, fussy phases are also likely to have less of an impact on the number of foods your child eats, especially over time; whereas not exposing them to different foods means they aren't able to grow to like them or accept them again on another day.

5. Make mealtimes fun

Take a look at your toddler's mealtimes: Are they pressured? Have they become a battleground? Are they stressful occasions? Is your child eating alone and looking for attention?

If your toddler doesn't enjoy mealtimes, it is going to have a knock-on effect on how they like their foods. Think about how mealtimes can be more of a pleasant and enjoyable experience for all, even if this means not focusing on the food being eaten for the time being.

Making mealtimes fun often means ticking off points 1–3: sitting together, listening to your toddler's needs and avoiding pressure at mealtimes.

DEVELOPING A POSITIVE RELATIONSHIP WITH FOOD

1

The first years of a child's life are really quite exceptional. Children learn so much during this time, including new social skills and how to communicate, alongside rapid growth and brain development. At the same time, they transition from a milk-only diet to a complex diet similar to ours as adults. All this in a matter of just a few years!

It's really no surprise, then, that raising toddlers can be a bit of a minefield. Most of us are really trying our best, but having so much information available about the 'right' way to parent or what we 'should' be doing to raise happy kids can lead to feelings of guilt and failure. I know – I've been there myself! Trials and errors are going to be part of the journey of raising children and quite often the challenges that can come with toddlerhood can have a knock-on effect on their eating behaviours too. I have found with my own kids – as well as from speaking to so many other parents – that when emotions are running high or there is any problem, appetite is usually the first thing to go!

If you think about it, we expect kids to learn to walk, talk and run gradually, not from the moment they take their first step or say their first word. The same is true with healthy eating – children need to learn the 'what' and 'how' of eating, and it might take them a few years to perfect the art of eating a balanced and varied diet (see Chapter 2). However, we can help to shape children's eating behaviours and food preferences when they are young.

As Giles Yeo, a geneticist from the University of Cambridge, says:

'Genes play a key role in influencing our feeding behaviour ... but your food environment, how you're fed, the foods you're exposed to ... and the role models you have in life are more likely to influence how you ultimately eat'

What Influences Children's Eating?

In the early years, children discover what they enjoy eating; they learn patterns of eating, pick up food preferences and even learn social skills and cultural norms around how and what to eat. Importantly, all this tends to track into late childhood and into adulthood, meaning that **promoting positive eating behaviours now in the early years can support positive relationships with food later on.**

However, children are complex, and multiple factors will influence what they choose to eat throughout their lives. Some of these are shown on the diagram below. As you can see, so many factors influence children's eating, but we're only really interested in the ones we can change (shown in bold) to support our little ones to enjoy food and learn to eat well.

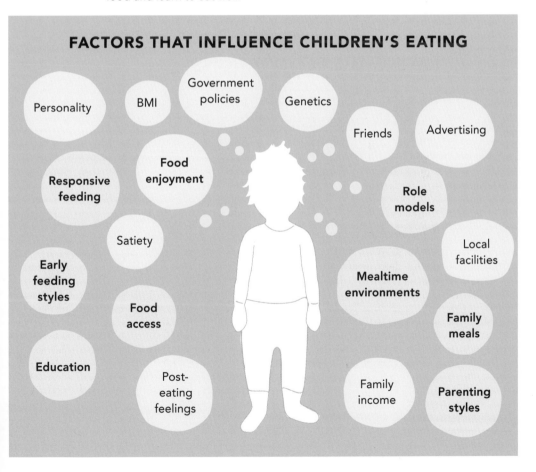

FACTORS THAT INFLUENCE CHILDREN'S EATING

Personality — BMI — Government policies — Genetics — Friends — Advertising — **Responsive feeding** — **Food enjoyment** — **Role models** — Satiety — Local facilities — **Early feeding styles** — **Mealtime environments** — **Food access** — **Family meals** — Education — **Post-eating feelings** — Family income — **Parenting styles**

How to Raise a Little Foodie

In writing this book, I did a huge amount of research into how we as parents can help to positively shape our children's food preferences in their early years. It goes something like this:

1. Laying the foundations

2. Parental influence

3. Mealtime environments

4. Extra strategies

5. Feedback from your child

These all take time and are dependent on consistency and being persistent with using them. However, an overarching factor is being super responsive to feedback from your child at food/mealtimes. This is known as 'responsive feeding' and I cover it in detail on page 34.

 ## LAYING THE FOUNDATIONS

This really means you, as a parent or carer, trying to:

Create a predictable structure. Young children thrive off routine – I know my two do – and if children know when to expect their foods it can really help them to understand, learn and tune into their own signs of hunger and fullness.

Make healthy food available. Offer foods that are balanced, varied, safe and appropriate for their age (see Chapter 2).

Support them to eat well. Help to educate your toddler about food and where it comes from as part of their culture and day-to-day learning about the world.

HOW TO POSITIVELY INFLUENCE CHILDREN'S EATING

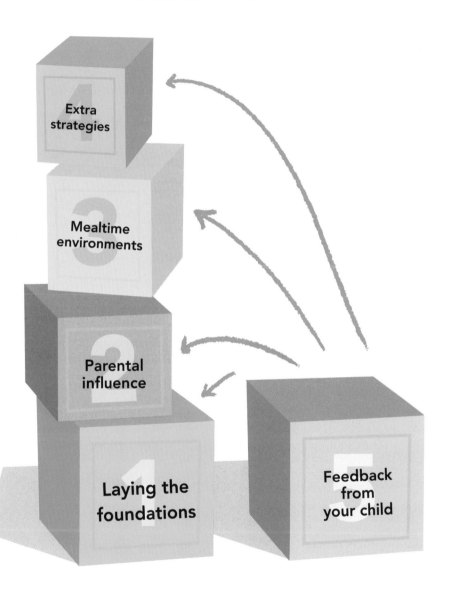

PARENTAL INFLUENCE

As our toddlers go through the early years, their eating is likely to be influenced by us as parents as well as others around them.

PARENTING STYLES

Often our language, restrictions, rules and behaviours around food can have a big impact on how children view food and mealtimes. As parents we use different tactics or strategies to try to get our kids to eat up and to encourage a healthy diet, and we all usually have different approaches to this depending on our 'parenting style'.

As you can see below, these four categories are very much generalisations and it's likely that at different times (and even different times of the day!) parents will tap into several parenting styles and techniques, and this is perfectly normal.

We're all different, and there is no judgement about the way that you parent here – it's all trial and error and about doing what works for you and your family. However, when it comes to feeding toddlers, there may be some parenting styles that work better than others at encouraging children to eat well, eat the right amounts for them and enjoy their foods.

INDULGENT STYLES

- Lack of control and structure at mealtimes.
- Giving children control over what and how much they eat.
- Little monitoring of how much is eaten.
- Acceptance and nurturing of exactly how they want to eat.

AUTHORITATIVE STYLES

- Offers a structure for meals.
- Includes mealtime rules that are explained to children.
- Mealtimes are warm and engaging.
- Interest in food is encouraged without pressure.
- Child decides how much they eat.
- Subtle praise and discussions around food.
- Responsive feeding practices.

AUTHORITARIAN STYLES

- Strict instructions on what can and can't be eaten.
- Lots of rewards or punishments used around foods.
- Pressure to 'eat up'.
- Overly restricting certain foods.
- Little negotiation about mealtime rules and children not making choices.

UNINVOLVED STYLES

- Parents aren't responsive or demanding.
- Little engagement from the parent around food, eating or mealtimes.
- Children are somewhat left to their own devices.
- Disorganised and unstructured mealtimes.

A positive approach to feeding

From all of the research, it seems that picking up some positive elements from the 'authoritative' parenting style could be helpful when feeding toddlers. This might look like having a certain time of day when food is offered and establishing rules such as 'we eat at the table, eat together and ask before we get down'. At the same time, children should have some autonomy over the meal – they should be able to say if they have had enough or would like seconds, and have a parent respond appropriately to that request.

HELPFUL PARENTING STYLES AT MEALTIMES

If we can strive towards some of these techniques, it could help to create a child who listens to their own internal cues but is also familiar with, and accepting of, a balance and variety.

Some mealtime rules

Creating routine

Encouraging interest

Explanations and discussions

Supportive

Responsive feeding

Offering independence

Nurturing

Structure

Sensitive

Involving child

OTHER WAYS PARENTS INFLUENCE EATING

It's so easy for mealtimes to become fraught after years of trying to get kids to eat well with you, making delicious hot dinners that are refused, and everyone feeling super tired after a long day at work/nursery. However, mealtime pressure has been shown to lessen children's responsiveness to their own needs. For example, strict instructions such as 'Finish what's on your plate' or 'You're not having any pudding until you've eaten all of your broccoli' (don't worry, we've all done it!) can actually overrule children's own hunger and fullness feelings, and are likely to stop them responding so well to them in the long run.

There is a big difference between controlling the what, the where and the how much of a child's eating and helping them to learn about the importance of balance and health through limiting the regular access of some foods and showing moderation via role modelling.

Role modelling

Children copy so much of what we do – our words, our actions, how we interact with each other – and that includes the how, what and why of our food choices, and even attitudes to food:

- **Modelling:** A lot of evidence highlights that this is key to encouraging children to eat well. In fact, some studies indicate that if we're trying to improve dietary intakes in young children, we should focus on improving the parent's intakes first and, as a knock-on effect, the toddler's diet is likely to improve too! Win-win, I say.

- **Eating together:** It has been shown that letting children see us eat a wide variety at mealtimes, including portions of fruit and veg, provides a valuable opportunity to help encourage them to eat well, eat a variety, eat more fruit and veg and enjoy foods too.

- **Teach moderation:** Research shows that children whose parents ate snack foods considered less healthy typically ate more of these foods themselves. I'm not saying to avoid these foods completely, but instead teach little ones about moderation by modelling what that looks like and avoiding a 'do as I say, not as I do' approach.

- **Peer role modelling:** This is especially important if children are sociable and/or have friends who they look up to. This is likely to be one of the reasons why so many families I work with find that their toddler eats well at nursery, but not so much at home!

Food language and food 'rules'

Our own attitude towards food and health can impact our children's attitudes too. For example, having attitudes to food such as 'carbs are bad', displaying dieting practices and even allowing them to see and hear about our own body hang-ups can all easily be picked up and adopted by our little ones. This emphasises why the language we use around our children in relation to food is so important.

Even on the topic of fussy eating (which we will cover later), this is key. Telling children 'You won't like this' or commenting to friends and family 'He doesn't eat anything; he's so fussy' in front of them is likely to become embedded over time and impact on the way they form their relationships with food. Instead, I like to keep food language positive or neutral, as shown below.

SWITCHING AROUND THE LANGUAGE

✖ INSTEAD OF...	♥ TRY...
'Sugar is bad for you.'	'It's always important to have a variety of foods, not just cake.'
'I can't eat that – I'll get fat.'	'I'm OK – I don't feel like eating that today.'
'You're so fussy with food.'	'It's OK if you don't feel like eating much today.'
'Broccoli is gross.'	'Broccoli is not my favourite, but I do love courgette.'
'I'm going on a diet.'	'I'd like to eat more variety this week.'
'Just have one more spoonful.'	'It's your choice how much you eat – try to listen to your tummy and let me know when you've had enough.'

Food rewards and treats

A really common parenting practice to get kids to eat up has been to offer rewards for eating. However, the general consensus from research is that using food rewards is unhelpful. 'If you eat X you will get Y' seems to lead to children regularly wanting the hit from the more desirable reward food!

Research on offering non-food rewards is mixed. However, though non-food rewards might work well for children who are generally motivated by rewards, for other children they may be interpreted as pressure. If your approach is consistent and (very importantly) doesn't encourage your little one to feel pressured to eat or lead to even more of a dislike of a certain food, then it could be helpful for your family to use some non-food rewards – such as praise, positive attention or stickers – as a way of helping them learn to enjoy more foods, especially vegetables.

Similarly, offering food as a reward or a treat suggests that some foods are 'good' and others 'bad', and it would be better to avoid separating food into these two categories. Encouraging conversations that suggest that foods are all 'level pegging' as much as you can and for as long as you can is ideal.

This helps to lessen the 'food hierarchy' that can make foods high in sugar and salt (often the ones with very little nutrients in them too) the gold standard in the food kingdom. Let's be realistic – parties and celebrations are likely to be all about the sweet food and cakes; but this is about helping children, especially in the early years when they are learning about their food environment, to adopt healthy patterns of eating and varied food preferences for the long term.

AVOIDING FOOD HIERARCHIES

Ways I've tried to put foods on a level playing field with my own kids include:

- Not overly restricting sweet foods once kids are aware of them.

- Offering sweet foods as part of a meal, rather than after as a 'pudding'.

- Not drawing attention to foods such as cake and crisps above other foods, for example avoiding phrasing such as 'Oh, how lucky, you got a cake!'

- Talking about and emphasising the need for variety rather than restricting how much they eat at any occasion.

- Allowing them to eat in the order they want and not capping how much at a particular sitting.

- Talking about the enjoyment of eating all foods, not just sweet foods.

- Educating on 'balance' and how some foods might make us feel a bit unwell if we eat too much of them.

- Encouraging them to listen to their tummies and how they feel and to stop when full.

3 MEALTIME ENVIRONMENTS

The environment in which our children eat can have a huge impact on how they feel about food. If it is a less positive environment, there is pressure to 'eat up'. When meals end up being stressful times of the day, children will be less likely to want to be a part of them. Making mealtimes enjoyable, engaging places for children, where they feel heard and where family members tend to be calm, is more likely to lead to children wanting to be a part of them and engaging in conversation as well as the food.

Mealtimes are a great way to teach children what food is all about! They'll learn from watching you whether food is a joy or simply a necessity. They'll also experience watching those around them try a variety and will learn the social aspects of eating too. This is why spending mealtimes together, as much as you can, can be really key for helping kids to learn to love their food.

Remember, it doesn't have to be every single meal and every single family member, but research does show that there is a positive association between the number of family meals eaten together and healthier eating patterns of children. Childminders, grandparents, siblings or friends eating together is just as great! And when it comes to having the TV on or using screens at mealtimes, this can really distract – we want mealtimes to be a time when food is the main focus to help children learn to enjoy what they're eating.

If you ever feel like your family mealtimes aren't quite working, take a step back and try to see why that might be:

- Have they become fractured?
- Are they negative environments?
- Is your toddler distracted?

If so, see if you can make a change – sometimes a little tweak to the mealtime environment can make all the difference to how your child enjoys their food.

FOR BETTER MEALTIMES...

✖ INSTEAD OF...	♥ TRY...
Everyone having separate meals	Eating together
Eating foods that your toddler can't eat in front of them	Eating similar foods regularly
Pressure to eat up, following rules or having to eat in a certain way or order	Non-pressured eating
Restricting pudding if other things are not eaten	Allowing child autonomy over how much is eaten and not using food as a reward or punishment (such as restricting pudding)
Lack of structure or routine around the mealtimes	Having a structure to mealtimes
Offering no say or choice in foods offered	Getting them involved in mealtimes and giving some choice between A and B
Commenting negatively on uneaten food	Positive discussions around the table
Offering multiple alternatives to the meal on offer	Offering plenty of variety within a meal, including some things your toddler does like
Arguing around the table, especially about food	Calm, unrushed mealtimes, not always focused on food
Waiting at the table when food isn't ready	Offering food at a time when your little one is likely to be hungry
Coaxing, bribing or cajoling into eating	Talk about hunger and fullness signs

MY TOP TIPS FOR HAPPY MEALTIME ENVIRONMENTS...

1. Offer colourful meals, including a variety of foods.

2. Eat together as much as you can.

3. Avoid pressure and focus on making the mealtime enjoyable.

4. Allow your toddler to eat to appetite.

5. Try playing some gentle music in the background.

6. Get your little one involved in helping to prep for the meal by laying the table, chopping, stirring or choosing what's on offer from 'A' or 'B' menu.

7. Kick off with a game or play musical bumps to decide where you'll all sit.

8. Have a routine around meals to ensure hunger, but not over-hunger.

9. Chat and engage your toddler in conversation, not always about food.

10. Try listing things you're grateful for or ask what their favourite part of the day has been. Share yours too.

EXTRA STRATEGIES

Below are some extra tips that you can try to help make food enjoyable, varied and something your toddler wants to get involved with. Not all of these will work for every child – sometimes it's about a little trial and error.

- **Offer little extras:** I'm such a fan of adding extras to top up and bulk out meals with nutrients: a sprinkle of milled seeds here, a handful of peas there.

- **Try buffet-style eating:** This can take the pressure off kids to 'finish their plate' and help them to have some autonomy over what they select. Buffets also allow them to be visually exposed to variety, even if they don't eat it initially (this still helps with familiarisation).

- **Serve a dip with veggies:** Some research shows that offering a dip alongside veggies can help kids to eat a little more of the veggies – even those disliked ones.

- **Offer accepted foods with new foods:** Research shows that offering a new flavour with a food that's already been accepted by a child can help them to be more accepting of the new food. Once they've accepted the new flavour, it's good to offer it on its own too, not only paired with something else.

- **Offer veggies as a starter:** Some research suggests that starting with a small plate of veggies might increase veggie intakes overall.

- **Get them involved:** You can familiarise kids with foods by doing more than serving them up. Research shows that doing activities such as growing food, cooking food or playing with and reading about food can help too.

- **Keep trying:** Persistence and consistency are always key!

Repeated exposures

Research has shown that offering children multiple opportunities to try foods can help them to become more familiar with those foods and that familiarisation is what can lead to acceptance. Therefore, it makes sense that repeatedly offering foods (without forcing or pressure) regularly, including offering them in different ways, can help to increase a toddler's acceptance and liking of them. This even includes foods that children initially point-blank refuse. It can take up to and beyond 15 'exposures' before certain foods will be accepted. Often this is the case with more savoury and bitter vegetables, but it can also be true with other foods too.

Offering repeated exposures doesn't mean forcing your toddler or offering the same rejected foods every day; it simply means that you don't need to write off foods or put them on the 'doesn't like' list too soon. Instead, it's a good idea to keep offering them gently, alongside other accepted foods and as part of your normal family meals. You might find it useful to use the chart opposite to encourage you to keep offering your little one rejected foods and keep a track of how many times they have been 'exposed' to them. Bear in mind that sometimes it might take more than 15 goes and that can be perfectly normal. And, of course, sometimes they are never going to grow to accept some foods, and that's OK too. Repeated exposures don't have to be all about eating foods either. Here are some of the ways you can help your child become familiar with foods before you even think about getting them to eat them:

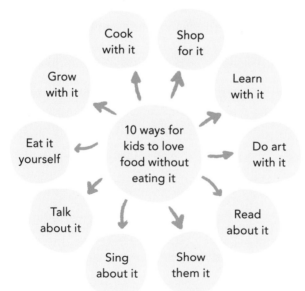

Cook with it

Shop for it

Grow with it

Learn with it

Eat it yourself

10 ways for kids to love food without eating it

Do art with it

Talk about it

Read about it

Sing about it

Show them it

FOOD	1	2	3	4	5	6	7	8	9	10	11	12	13	14	15	Accepted
Broccoli																✓
Egg																
Beef																
....																
....																
....																
....																
....																
....																
....																
....																
....																

5 FEEDBACK FROM YOUR CHILD

You can put all the strategies into place, offer a routine, adapt your parenting style and try to make mealtimes a joy, but if you're not actually listening and responding to your individual child – their feedback, their needs and their desires – a lot of this won't really work.

Feeding kids is also about being responsive to what works and what simply doesn't, and adapting when needed; letting your little one have some control; and encouraging them to listen to their own internal signals that tell them if they need more or less, or if they just don't feel like eating that meal/food today, for example.

There are government guidelines and recommendations when it comes to childhood nutrition, which you'll see throughout Chapter 2 (see pages 48–89), but it's up to us as parents to take these guidelines and adapt them, where necessary, for our family and our toddlers.

Until I had my own kids I recommended the guidance of three meals and two snacks a day as standard to parents. However, Raffy didn't need snacks. He ate big meals and enjoyed them! Snacks simply acted as an appetite suppressant. Ada was completely the opposite. She ate small amounts and needed 'mini meals' in between to help top her up. In these situations, I took on board the guidance and then saw how it worked for my children.

Responsive feeding

The idea behind 'responsive feeding' is to help your child learn to follow their own appetite and eat with autonomy, as well as to support them in learning to eat healthily for themselves.

Typically we see a lot of 'encouragement' for children to eat up at mealtimes and this can be interpreted by children as pressure. However, even gentle encouragement with phrases such as 'Just one more spoonful' may actually stop them from responding and listening to their own body signals, may stop them enjoying their food and may even teach them to overeat. Instead, follow the saying by Ellyn Satter, which goes:

> 'You decide what they eat and let
> them decide how much'

It can be hard to feed children responsively as many parents are worried that their little ones might go hungry, eat to excess or end up wasting lots of food. There will be times when appetites take a dive or when your kids don't want to eat the meals you're offering, and that's OK. It's *so* important not to just look at what they are eating over one meal or even a couple of meals. A few days or a week is a better indicator of children's eating behaviours and how much they are consuming.

Additionally, to practise responsive feeding, we can:

- **Try not to over-restrict certain foods:** Overly and obviously restricting access to some foods (once children are older and more aware), like cakes, puddings and sweet options, may actually increase a child's desire for these types of foods.

- **Communicate:** This is so key in responsive feeding so you both understand how mealtimes work and parents/carers set the pace and offer the structure, but children also have their own autonomy around meals. It takes a while to get to grips with this practice, but it can help to follow their lead and offer them autonomy around how much they eat from the start.

Coping with Fussy Eating

Fussy eating is a big issue for many parents and so I want you to know that you're not alone if you're finding your child's food refusal challenging. As a parent, part of your instinct is to feed your child to ensure they survive – 'I need my child to eat and so I'm going to do whatever it takes to make that happen' – and this is really common and understandable. However, this can often be what makes fussy eating harder than it needs to be or more prolonged. Sometimes the way we want to react is not the way that is likely to help fussy or picky eating to go away. So often there is mealtime conflict around food that can last weeks, months or even years.

A toddler's eating (or lack of) can take its toll on families. To help parents navigate this tricky time it's worth keeping in mind that some fussy behaviours are actually just normal peaks and troughs in the appetites of young children. I want to give you confidence to try to nip it in the bud early and avoid mealtimes becoming a battleground.

A lot of the information I've covered already in this chapter can help to keep fussy eating and food refusal at bay. However, I know from my own experience that there will likely be periods of food refusal, meals that go uneaten and sometimes (often for weeks on end) specific foods or whole food groups that are avoided. This can be very normal and absolutely part of many children's feeding journey.

LABELLING A 'FUSSY EATER'

Quite often, I see parents labelling their children as being 'fussy' with foods, when actually it may just be children exhibiting normal variations in their day-to-day appetite. Labelling it as 'fussy eating' almost suggests that children are not behaving as they should, and sometimes encourages us, as parents, to focus on 'fixing' it. This means we often employ tactics to try to encourage children to 'behave' at mealtimes, such as coaxing, pressuring or controlling, which in turn can lead to mealtime stress and children being less willing to eat the food on offer. It's actually a vicious cycle!

Instead, if we're able to remember that there are several reasons why children's appetites will vary day to day and allow a bit more autonomy with their own appetites, the opposite can be seen.

Additionally, we need to be careful when using terms such as 'fussy eater' in front of our children. This kind of label can stick and it can alter how you behave towards them at mealtimes and how others react or present food to them too. As we've already seen, if you talk about their fussy behaviours in front of them, it can actually have a knock-on effect on how they view their own relationship with food. If you're told from a young age 'You're so fussy', guess what? You're more likely to be so.

Put it into context

Before you start to worry about your child's food intake, it's always important to look at the bigger picture.

Look at your child's intake over a few days or a week, rather than taking the experience from a single meal. How did they eat:

- At breakfast?
- Yesterday at nursery?
- At the weekend?
- Last week?

It's so easy for us to focus on the negative, but context really matters with fussy eating.

INSTEAD OF...

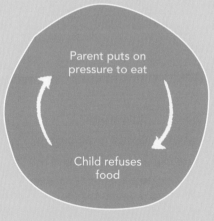

Parent puts on pressure to eat

Child refuses food

TRY...

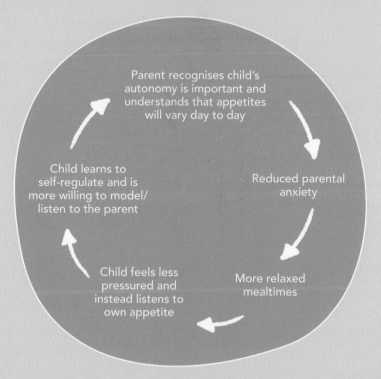

Parent recognises child's autonomy is important and understands that appetites will vary day to day

Reduced parental anxiety

More relaxed mealtimes

Child feels less pressured and instead listens to own appetite

Child learns to self-regulate and is more willing to model/listen to the parent

PUTTING FUSSY EATING INTO CONTEXT

Look outside of this moment of food refusal and this specific mealtime and see if there is a reason why, right now, they don't want their meal...

Maybe they are feeling a little unwell?

Maybe they just aren't hungry?

Maybe they were expecting something else on their plate?

Maybe they wanted hot food and got a cold option instead?

Maybe we're expecting them to eat more than they actually need?

Maybe they had something similar at lunch?

WHAT ACTUALLY IS FUSSY EATING?

What do we actually mean by 'fussy eating'? The answer to this question is so subjective. For example, for one person, their child might be exhibiting fussy behaviour when for a few weeks they refuse to eat their broccoli. For another, they might be worried that their toddler is fussy if they eat no meals at all for three days straight. What it looks like is going to vary depending on your context, your child's eating to date and the experience of others around you. There is also no set definition of what 'fussy eating' is in research.

HOW DO I KNOW I HAVE A 'FUSSY EATER'?

Does your child...	YES	NO
Eat a different meal to the rest of the family?		
Have definite likes and dislikes when it comes to food?		
Have an obvious dislike towards new foods?		
Have a limited intake of foods?		
Eat a limited variety of foods?		
Show little enjoyment of food?		
Become stressed, anxious or upset at mealtimes?		
Seem 'very choosy' about what they will eat on a regular basis?		

If you've answered 'yes' to many of the questions above, it could be indicative that your child might be becoming quite selective with their foods and may need a little help to improve the variety they will eat.

Of course, sometimes children can show more extreme behaviours when it comes to food refusal. There can be a real spectrum of fussy eating, from mild to more severe cases, and the more severe cases will need further support from a multidisciplinary team. For example, if your little one shows a real disgust towards a lot of foods, eats a really limited diet which has been going on for months, seems to have a sensory aversion to certain foods/textures (which may be a condition called ARFID – Avoidant and Restrictive Food Intake Disorder), or is lacking in energy and experiencing slowed growth rate, then it's time to get some specialised support as these more extreme conditions are beyond the remit of this book.

A BIT OF REASSURANCE...

Although there is some research that suggests that fussy eating *may* put children at more of a risk of being either over- or underweight, it seems that health risks associated with *typical* fussy eating are pretty low. For example, though children who eat fewer fruit and veggies (especially veggies) and fewer whole grains, fish and meat may be lower in vitamin E, folate and fibre, research seems to suggest that child growth isn't hugely affected and, quite surprisingly, there are very few studies that actually show that *typical* fussy eating leads to any specific nutrient deficiencies. If you're ever worried or unsure, it's always best to ask your GP or health visitor, who can support you with checking your child's weight, food intake and offer any referrals, if needed.

When Raffy turned three, we started having problems with food refusal. Comments such as 'I don't like X' started cropping up when previously he'd loved everything, and sometimes he just wouldn't touch anything on his plate or would ask to leave the table. Even though this is what I've supported parents with my whole career, it took a while before I was able to digest what was happening and then roll out my own tried-and-tested, evidence-backed advice. Once I did, the refusal was short-lived and began to phase out. Phew.

WHY FUSSY EATING HAPPENS

Though fussy eating typically occurs around the age of eighteen months to three years, I get lots of families coming to me with children under one as well as with much older children where fussiness at mealtimes is causing concerns. As with everything, patterns of eating can start to stick and become 'the norm' in early childhood, which is why this age is an ideal time to help nip food refusal in the bud. It's thought to occur largely due to a few reasons:

Growth rate slowing

Children double their weight in the first year of life and during this time they grow faster than at any other time of their lives. However, the rate of growth peaks at around two years of age and then starts to slow down between the ages of two and five. With this can often come – you guessed it! – a reduction in appetite. So sometimes children's apparent 'fussy' behaviour can also coincide with a time when they may simply need less food. This is another great reason why it's best to pay attention to feedback from your little one and their own individual appetite cues.

Food neophobia

'Food neophobia' or a fear of new foods (this can also include ones they've previously enjoyed), is thought to offer evolutionary benefits at a time when toddlers are becoming more mobile and independent – they start to refuse foods that they are unsure of and foods that could potentially be harmful to them. Many foods in nature, especially bitter-tasting ones, contain toxins, so it makes sense, historically, for toddlers to be a bit more wary about what goes into their mouths (though it still baffles me why my daughter often refuses broccoli but will shovel handfuls of mud and stones into her mouth!).

Becoming independent

Sometimes children like to have some control over their own lives, and at this age they are starting to develop a bit of independence and autonomy. This can manifest in control around what they do and don't eat at mealtimes.

Fluctuations in appetite

One thing that is really key to know is that toddlers' appetites will vary a lot and that is perfectly normal. Up-and-down variations in what, how much and how often they want to eat show that our little ones are listening to their own intuition when it comes to food – and that's a good thing!

It's so important for us as parents to listen to their cues around their own appetite (only they know!) and let them decide how much they want to eat at any given mealtime.

Just like us adults, it's important to realise that kids will have their own feelings at mealtimes and sometimes be in the mood for rice, for example, and other times less so. It's hard for them to always communicate these desires with us and instead it comes out simply as 'I don't like it'.

A lot of these reasons are simply normal developmental changes that happen as children grow up. On top of this, most tend to grow out of fussy eating – possibly due to familiarisation, role models at school, exposure to a wide range of food and growing independence around food – and most children who are 'fussy eaters' tend to still get enough energy and nutrients in their diet to grow and develop properly.

OFFERING ALTERNATIVE MEALS

Ideally it's not a good idea to offer alternatives at mealtimes if foods are refused. If children let us know they don't want food, it might be because they simply aren't hungry. It's possible that by offering an alternative we show them that this is the way we deal with being not hungry and teach them to ignore their own appetite signals and eat something anyway, especially if they are being offered firm favourites as alternatives. Additionally, in my experience, the more alternatives offered, the more children start to refuse meals, until just a small handful of meals are easily accepted. This can reduce the variety that your child is exposed to, lead to you prepping more than one food option and reducing the opportunity for your toddler to share in family meals.

If this happens on the odd occasion, it's unlikely to be a problem, and if happens as a result of your toddler really not enjoying a new flavour or a new recipe, then offering an alternative as a one-off is fine to do. If you're worried about your little one missing a meal, try to remember that:

- They have multiple opportunities to eat throughout the day.

- It's unlikely that missing one meal will have much impact.

- It won't necessarily lead to them waking hungry during the night.

- If it becomes regular and it affects their night-time sleeping, you could try offering a small, balanced snack before bedtime as a regular part of their mealtime routine. This should be offered whether the dinner is refused or not.

> ### MY BIGGEST TIP:
>
> Pretend you don't care if your child eats the food or not, but show (subtly!) that you are excited and happy that you're getting to eat your own meal.

WHAT CAN YOU DO?

If you feel you're already in the throes of fussy eating or mealtimes have started to become a bit of a battleground, there are some extra strategies that you can employ to get you back on track with happy mealtimes.

IF YOUR MEALTIMES HAVE BECOME STRESSFUL

Think about making mealtimes calmer environments, especially if they've been getting stressful of late.

•

Stick to a routine around meals and snacks so your toddler can build up an appetite and knows when to expect foods during the day.

•

If mealtimes aren't something that your little one is keen on being at, stick to 20-minute meals max and stop the meal at any point if they are unhappy or crying.

•

Try changing up their positioning at the table for mealtimes for a change of scene.

•

Try some calming music or make the atmosphere more child-friendly with a colourful tablecloth or plate and cup of their choice.

•

Offer foods buffet-style so your child can have control over what they want to put on their plate.

IF YOU FEEL LIKE YOU HAVE TO COAX OR PRESSURE YOUR TODDLER TO EAT AT MEALTIMES

Pretend you don't care if they eat the food on offer. Sometimes this can help take the pressure off and allow them to feel much more empowered.

•

Try to allow them (however much this goes against your instinct!) to say no to something they don't want. Practise responsive feeding and let them listen to their appetite cues instead (see page 34).

•

Focus on making mealtimes enjoyable over getting them to eat (unless weight is a concern, in which case it's important to get some specialist support).

•

Offer smaller portions if your little one doesn't seem keen on meals.

•

Avoid overly focusing on food at mealtimes and try to focus on other discussions or simply enjoying your own meal.

•

Avoid commenting on, or drawing attention to, unwanted foods or foods that have been uneaten at the mealtime.

IF YOUR TODDLER IS STARTING TO REFUSE MORE AND MORE FOODS

Avoid offering alternatives if foods are refused as this can actually increase the likelihood of more and more foods being refused.

•

Get them to help with cooking and prepping the meals, even if it's laying the table or spreading a little butter on the bread.

•

Give them choices before the meal – just an A or B option can help.

•

Keep up with offering a variety to increase familiarity.

•

Try presenting foods in fun ways or making the foods look appealing. Try naming foods – such as 'Super Green Beans' or 'Barney Banana'.

•

Listen to feedback from your child during mealtimes.

MY MEALTIME FOOD REFUSAL GUIDE

1 Offer a balanced meal at a time when your toddler is likely to be hungry.

2 Offer some foods they are likely to eat alongside some food they may not eat or even try.

3 Avoid making any comment on the food, previous experiences and whether it's likely to be eaten before or during the meal.

4 Serve the same dish for yourself and anyone else at the table. Allow people to comment positively if they want to, but avoid overly emphasising what's on the plate.

5 If your child comments negatively on the meal or the food, simply reply, 'That's OK, you don't have to eat it.' Change the subject and if they ask you to remove the food from the plate, do so.

6 Allow them to eat as much or as little as they like from the plate and offer more of any parts of the meal they do like and ask for, if you have it.

7 Avoid offering alternatives if food is refused. Offering something else might encourage more foods to be refused on another day. A simple 'That's OK, you don't have to eat it' is again ideal.

8 Keep the mealtime as light and enjoyable as you can.

9 Clear away plates at the end of the meal and avoid commenting on the food left over.

10 Offer the rejected food(s) again at some point in the near future and continue to offer a wide variety of other foods generally to your toddler.

11 Don't worry if this doesn't work right away. These things take time – sometimes lots of time – but being consistent with this mealtime approach is key.

GETTING THE BALANCE RIGHT

2

Toddlers growing in independence like to find control in a life that they generally have little control over. This may be reflected in behaviours around refusing bath time, teeth brushing or putting on clothes and… yes, you guessed it, having a say in the foods they will or won't eat! It's part of the package of feeding toddlers, and although we can't (and shouldn't) ever force children to eat, they are still very much dependent on us to provide them with a healthy and balanced diet.

We can help them by laying down the foundations of a balanced diet and offering mealtime structure so they can learn how to enjoy food and patterns of eating that are likely to be beneficial for them now and into their futures.

We hear the words 'healthy, balanced diet' bandied about all the time – but there are some very good reasons for this being the core message that nutritionists (like me) want people to take on board.

Ultimately, offering 'balance' to your child is all about getting the right levels of energy and nutrients into their diet that they need to grow and develop well. The nutritional requirements of children between the ages of one and four are quite different to those of older children and adults – mainly because toddlers have small stomachs, are growing fast and have high energy and nutrient needs relative to their small body sizes.

Therefore, we need to make the most out of the foods they do eat and ensure that they are topping up their levels of energy and nutrients wherever possible, while also learning to enjoy foods and develop important skills around eating.

Of course, measuring the nutrients in your little one's daily foods is nigh on impossible, so instead we recommend a 'balanced diet'. In this chapter I'll show you why that's so important, as well as how to get the balance right with some easy, practical tips.

Studies show children in the UK have diets that are too high in sugar and too low in fruit and veg.

What Is a Balanced Diet?

Balancing your toddler's diet essentially means offering foods each day from each of the food groups, in the rough proportions and number of servings represented here:*

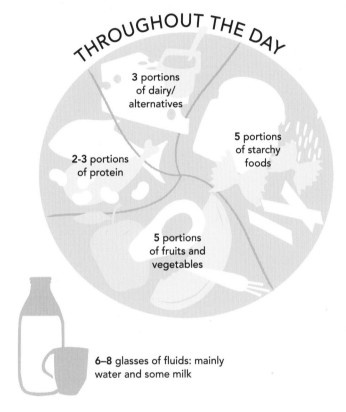

THROUGHOUT THE DAY

3 portions of dairy/ alternatives

5 portions of starchy foods

2-3 portions of protein

5 portions of fruits and vegetables

6–8 glasses of fluids: mainly water and some milk

Provide a balance of foods over the day in meals and snacks, roughly in these proportions.

The only real difference between a balanced diet for adults and children is that kids will likely need smaller portions of foods, but as they are growing at a rapid rate they need more energy and nutrients per mouthful.

*Graphic based on the Eatwell Guide, adapted for ages 1–4, and the British Nutrition Foundation's '5532' guidelines

VEGETABLES AND FRUITS

Fill one-third of your toddler's plate with fruits and veggies and offer around five portions a day – ideally at each meal and for any snacks too. Try to think about offering a variety of fruit and veg, including a variety of colours (see page 56). Fruit and vegetables are full of fibre, vitamins, minerals and water, and so much research promotes the benefits of offering these in abundance in children's and adult's diets.

- Includes all fresh, frozen and tinned (as long as tinned in water or natural juices and not salted water and syrups) fruits and vegetables like broccoli, kale, nectarines, bananas and berries.

- Includes beans and pulses, but these only count once as they have a different nutritional make-up to other fruits and vegetables, and because they also count towards intakes from the protein food group (see page 55).

- Potatoes are considered more of a starchy food and so aren't counted in the fruit and veggie portions.

- Dried fruits are only recommended to be offered with meals due to the impact they can have on little one's teeth as they are sticky and a concentrated form of sugar.

- Fruit juice can count towards fruit and veg portions, but there are stipulations (see page 76).

The more variety of these foods, the better, so think outside the box and try not to get stuck offering just the same ones each day!

STARCHY FOODS

These are carbohydrate foods and should make up around one-third of your toddler's plate. These foods contain energy, which growing kids need a lot of, and they also contain fibre, B vitamins, iron and protein, to name just a few nutrients.

- Includes whole grains, which means the food has been made with the whole part of the grain and hasn't had any of its elements stripped. Wholegrain foods include wholegrain bread and pasta and brown rice.

- Includes breads, chapattis, rice, potatoes, sweet potatoes, pasta, couscous, quinoa, breakfast cereals, oats, polenta, yam, plantain, rye and millet.

Try to include at least one food from this food group with each meal, and you can also offer them as snacks.

For children under two, lots of high-fibre foods can bulk out their tummies and leave less room for foods from the other food groups. From two years of age you can gradually introduce more whole grains as children's growth slows and they move towards eating a diet similar to the recommendations for adults (eating a high-fibre diet and focusing mainly on wholegrain carbohydrates).

TIP: AIM FOR VARIETY

Variety is always key with these food groups, so if you find that your little one is having bread with every meal or only the same few vegetables each week, it's a good idea to try to increase the variety you're offering.

DAIRY FOODS AND ALTERNATIVES

Many toddlers are still having breast milk over the age of one as the World Health Organization (WHO) recommends breastfeeding until two years of age and beyond. If your little one is having plenty of breast milk (possibly around three or more feeds a day) then you may not need to offer cow's milk or alternative milks as a drink.

If you're not offering breast milk to your toddler, dairy foods or alternatives should be offered around three times a day. This includes: full-fat cow's milk, yoghurt and cheese, or non-dairy alternatives that are plain and (importantly) fortified. For more information on drinks for your toddler, see pages 76–80.

- These foods are a good source of calcium, protein, B vitamins, iodine and fat. As fat is important for growth in young children, it's recommended that full-fat versions of dairy foods are offered at least until they are two years of age.

- Offer plain varieties of dairy foods, such as unsweetened milk or plain or natural yoghurt, rather than flavoured options as these often have added sugars. Offering these may encourage your toddler to refuse the plain varieties and only eat the sweeter options.

- Avoid offering your little one unpasteurised milks as there is a higher risk of food poisoning as the milk hasn't been treated or heated to destroy any potential bacteria.

- Other animal milks such as goat's and sheep's can also be offered as a main drink once your baby is one year old, as long as they are pasteurised. They have a similar nutritional profile to cow's milk.

- If your child has an allergy or intolerance to milk or you'd like to offer non-dairy alternatives, opt for fortified, plain options where possible (see page 79). It can be helpful to speak to a healthcare professional about the best non-dairy options for your child.

PROTEIN-RICH FOODS

These foods are often a source of iron – a really important nutrient for young children – as well as protein, zinc, B vitamins, selenium and fats. Protein-rich foods include beans, lentils, pulses, peas, ground nuts and seeds, as well as fish, eggs, meat, poultry, tofu and some soya meat alternatives.

❁   These foods should be included around two to three times a day in children's diets – ideally three times if children are vegetarian or plant-based and/or don't eat any meat.

❁   Omega-3 fatty acids are also an important nutrient found within foods in this food group, mainly oily fish such as salmon, mackerel, herring and sardines. It's recommended that two small portions of fish should be eaten a week, one of which should be oily, in line with advice for adults (see page 70).

❁   It's ideal to limit processed meat and fish intakes (such as salami, ham, corned beef, bacon and smoked salmon) because they are highly processed and contain high levels of salt.

FOR VEGETARIANS AND VEGANS

When it comes to vegetarian or vegan options of protein- and iron-rich foods, the iron from these foods is less efficiently absorbed than the iron from meat sources. Therefore it's recommended to stick to offering three portions of plant-based protein and iron-rich options a day (rather than just two).

Colourful Foods

Fruits and veggies get hailed as these 'all-important' foods, but are they really?

○ Fruits and vegetables have unique health benefits to us as humans, and the evidence for this is growing all the time. Studies have found a strong link between higher intakes of different fruits and vegetables and a decreased risk of us getting ill from chronic diseases (such as cardiovascular disease, diabetes and cancer) in later life. There is a reason that the government and organisations such as the WHO and the World Cancer Research Fund have campaigns such as 'five-a-day' to encourage us to increase our consumption of fruit and veg.

○ It's likely that children who eat plenty of fruits and vegetables when they are young will carry on eating more of them as adults and this is where they can get many health benefits!

○ Fruits and vegetables contain a variety of vitamins and minerals, such as vitamin A, vitamin C, vitamin K and folate. They also contain lots of plant compounds often called 'phytochemicals' or 'antioxidants', and these are some of the important ingredients that are known to have beneficial effects on the cells in our bodies. This includes beta-carotene, which converts to vitamin A in the body and is found in orange and green fruits and veggies; lycopene, found in tomatoes; capsanthin in peppers; and also fibre, which is found in large quantities in most fruits and vegetables. All these different nutrients and plant properties are likely to offer a variety of benefits to the human body.

Focus on filling your little one's plate with a variety of colours from fruits and veggies, including red, blue, green, purple, orange, yellow, pink – the more the merrier! Not only can fruit and veg provide health benefits, but they also can make your kid's meals pop with vibrancy.

HOW TO BALANCE YOUR TODDLER'S MEALS

When thinking about how to balance your toddler's meals, it's all about adding foods from each of the food groups. So, start with some carbs, add some veg or fruit, include some iron and protein foods and then add some flavours and/or some dairy!

A BALANCED MEAL =

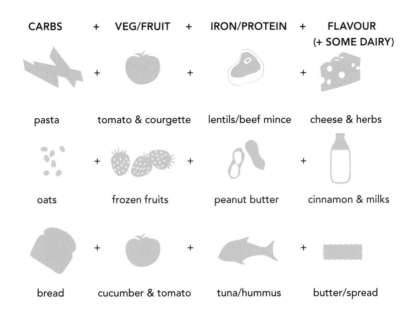

CARBS	+	VEG/FRUIT	+	IRON/PROTEIN	+	FLAVOUR (+ SOME DAIRY)
pasta		tomato & courgette		lentils/beef mince		cheese & herbs
oats		frozen fruits		peanut butter		cinnamon & milks
bread		cucumber & tomato		tuna/hummus		butter/spread

FIVE-A-DAY FOR KIDS

A toddler's palm-sized piece of fruit or veg is around one portion. Just aim for plenty of variety and around five different portions a day.

IMPORTANT NUTRIENTS FOR TODDLERS

There are a few nutrients that young children often fall short of in their diet (for example, iron, vitamin A and zinc) and there are also some that are incredibly important for children's growth and development. You can see some of both here. Remember, though: offering a well-balanced diet is all you really need to ensure your little one is getting enough of these.

FAT

Young children who have small tummies and are growing rapidly need plenty of calories (energy) in order to grow and develop properly, but also in order to run around, play and learn. Eating foods high in fat helps children to get enough energy from their food, but it's important they are eating plenty of nutrients too. For example, foods like olive oil, nuts and avocado contain some of the helpful fats that we want to include more of in our toddler's diet, but they also provide plenty of vitamins and minerals. Meanwhile, foods such as chocolate and cakes often contain lots of fats, but these tend to be the fats we want to eat less of and these foods don't usually provide much in the way of vitamins and minerals.

Practical ways to get fat in:

- Add rapeseed, olive or vegetable oil when cooking.

- Use dips such as yoghurt, hummus and guacamole when serving bread or veggie sticks.

- Add yoghurt or cheese to sauces.

- Stir nut butter or ground nuts into porridge and cereals.

OMEGA-3

This is a fat that comes mainly from oily fish, including salmon, trout, sardines and herring, which can sometimes be a struggle to get children to eat! Omega-3 is needed for brain health and eye development, and has been shown in research to also be important for a healthy heart.

Practical ways to get omega-3 in:

- Add fish as a toast topping or potato filling, or add chunks to pies and stews.

- If your child doesn't like or eat oily fish, include flaxseed oil, ground walnuts, chia seeds and omega-3-enriched eggs when cooking.

- Look for some fortified foods.

- If little omega-3-rich food is eaten, algae oils or supplements can provide a vegan source.

Foods labelled as 'low-fat' or 'diet' are not ideal for growing children.

FIBRE

Many young children's diets aren't high enough in fibre. Fibre is important for helping to prevent constipation and to look after their digestive systems. However, very young children (mainly those under two) can bulk out their tummies with lots of high-fibre foods, leaving less room for other foods, which can impact a balanced diet. The answer to this is to gradually increase the amount of fibre you offer to young children over time, presenting some whole grains and white carbohydrate when children are very young, but from the age of two gradually trying to introduce more whole grains alongside plenty of fruits and vegetables to ensure adequate fibre intake. When gradually increasing fibre intake, it's important to ensure young children are keeping well hydrated too. Beans, pulses, wholegrain carbohydrates (such as oats, brown rice and wholegrain bread/pasta) and fruits and vegetables all contain fibre.

Practical ways to get fibre in:

- Vary the types of carbohydrates you offer to your toddler and sometimes opt for wholegrain bread, rice and pasta.

- Add beans and lentils to main meals.

- Offer fruits and veggies on the side of main meals and as snacks.

IRON

Iron requirements are quite high in young children relative to their body size as iron is really important for growth. Children aged one to three years are recommended to have 6.9mg iron per day, in comparison to 6.1mg per day for four- to six-year-olds. Toddlers are one of the groups more at risk of iron deficiency due to the fact that they often don't consume enough iron-rich foods and sometimes have high intakes of dairy foods (which can displace iron-rich foods), and simply due to them having high iron needs. Therefore, it's important to include a variety of iron-containing food options, such as fortified cereals and some vegetables, as well as good sources of iron-rich foods such as meat, fish, egg yolks, lentils, ground nuts and tofu.

Practical ways to get iron in:

- Stir nut butters into cereals and porridge.

- Add lentils to sauces, soups and pizza toppings.

- Choose fortified breakfast cereals (check the ingredients list for iron).

- Offer meat- or tofu-based dishes.

VITAMIN A

This vitamin is important for young children's growth and eye health, and the UK government currently recommends a supplement for children under the age of five. Foods that contain vitamin A include dairy, eggs, oily fish, orange-coloured fruit and veg and dark-green leafy vegetables.

Practical ways to get vitamin A in:

- Choose plenty of orange fruits and veggies such as apricots, nectarines, carrots and yellow peppers.

- Use sweet potato as an occasional replacement for standard potatoes – make wedges or a jacket.

- Add spinach, cheese or eggs to dishes when cooking.

VITAMIN C

Vitamin C comes largely from fruits and vegetables in our diet and it's actually pretty easy to meet young children's requirements, especially if they are eating a balanced diet. However, the UK government does still recommend a supplement for children.

Practical ways to get vitamin C in:

- Throw a handful of fruit on cereal in the morning.

- Chop up veggie sticks and offer them at snack times.

- Use lemon juice to flavour foods, such as yoghurt, or drizzle it on salads or avocado.

- Offer broccoli on the side at dinnertime.

VITAMIN D

Vitamin D is actually a hormone and it's pretty hard to obtain from food alone. Vitamin D is important for healthy bones and teeth and so young children are especially vulnerable as they are growing pretty quickly. A lot of our vitamin D requirement is created in the body from direct sunlight; however, with variable levels of sun in the UK, quite a high proportion of the population has low vitamin D levels, and children are more likely to be covered up in the sun. The UK government therefore recommends a supplement for all children under the age of five.

Practical ways to get vitamin D in:

- Offer oily fish to your toddler once a week – sardines on toast or fish pie with salmon are good examples.

- Make sure you offer your little one their supplement each day.

Add some vitamin C-rich fruits and veggies, such as broccoli, oranges and red peppers, to your child's meals to help them absorb more iron.

 = supplement recommended

CALCIUM

Calcium is important for bone and teeth health as well as muscle function. Many children in the UK get a lot of their calcium from milk and dairy foods, and these are some of the main/highest sources of calcium. Offering a balanced diet including three portions of dairy foods a day should provide enough calcium, but if your little one doesn't eat dairy, you can offer a variety of plant-based sources such as calcium-set tofu, calcium-fortified plant milks, ground nuts and seeds, figs, beans, lentils, pulses, spinach and kale. Lots of plant foods contain plenty of calcium, just not in as high amounts as in dairy foods.

Practical ways to get calcium in:

- Stir cheese or yoghurts into soups and sauces.
- Add ground nuts and seeds to porridge and snacks.
- Add spinach and lentils to curries and soups.
- Offer a variety of fruits and vegetables each day.
- Look for foods that are fortified with calcium, for example some breakfast cereals and plant-based milks.

IODINE

In the UK, iodine comes largely from dairy foods, especially milk, and from fish. There are limited sources of iodine in other foods, so if your child doesn't eat meat or fish, it's a good idea to speak to a healthcare professional to check they are getting enough. Plant milk fortified with iodine (this is variable so do check labels) can be a good source, as can eggs and other iodine-fortified foods, though fortification with iodine is a little limited in the UK. Iodine is important for our thyroid, which helps with growth and brain development.

Practical ways to get iodine in:

- Choose plant milks that are specifically fortified with iodine (if you don't drink cow's milk).
- Add yoghurt and cheese to foods when cooking.
- Add fish to dishes you're cooking for the whole family.

In our house, both my kids love taking their supplements as we've always made a bit of a big deal out of it – 'Who wants their vitamin?', 'Who is going first?', 'Quick, Daddy is trying to steal them!'. We also get Raffy involved in administrating them himself (with supervision!), which he loves to do.

SUPPLEMENTS

The UK government currently recommends that young children from one to five years of age take the following supplements (as long as they are having less than 500ml of formula milk a day):

Vitamin D: Children are recommended to have around 10mcg a day of vitamin D, and the UK government recommends a 10mcg supplement is taken to achieve this, due to the limited sources from foods.

Vitamin A: The UK government currently recommends a supplement to top up intakes from food. The supplement doesn't need to cover all requirements (400mcg is recommended for children aged one to six), but needs to provide some of it. For example, the government's 'Healthy Start' vitamins provide 233mcg of Vitamin A.

Vitamin C: Children aged between one and ten are recommended to have 30mg of vitamin C a day: one medium-sized kiwi will provide more than that amount. However, it is recommended that all children aged one to five receive a supplement containing vitamin C, to ensure adequate intake.

MY TIPS FOR GETTING TODDLERS TO TAKE SUPPLEMENTS

✓ Start from the earliest age the supplement is recommended – the earlier you can introduce them the better so they become 'the norm'.

✓ Persevere with trying to offer them regularly, but avoid forcing your little one to take them and try to make it fun.

✓ Go for vitamin drops, which are often easier to administer.

✓ Add vitamin drops to your child's food or milk (cold foods only as heating may destroy some of the vitamins).

✓ If they are happy to, add vitamin drops under the tongue and make it a bit of a game for your toddler.

✓ If applicable, role model and show them you taking your own supplements at the same time.

MULTIVITAMINS

Multivitamins aren't really needed for young children, especially if they are being offered a well-balanced diet. Ideally, you just need to offer plenty of variety, alongside the recommended supplements to ensure they get all they need. However, if you're worried your toddler is getting a bit fussy about their foods or if they won't eat a certain food group, then it might be worth thinking about offering a multivitamin. It's important to remember that this isn't a replacement for a balanced diet, but it may act as a safeguard in case they are low in anything. It's important not to offer multiple supplements to toddlers, so have a chat with your healthcare professional or pharmacist about which multivitamins might be best.

If children are on plant-based or vegan diets, they may need to take supplements of vitamin B12, omega-3 and iodine (or consume foods that are fortified with these nutrients), and potentially others depending on their current dietary intake. It's always worth chatting to a registered nutritionist or dietitian directly if your little one is on a vegan diet, just to make sure they are getting the balance of nutrients they need.

If your child has multiple allergies it also might be worthwhile talking to your healthcare professional about which supplements would be most suitable for your child – they may well need a few extras, depending on their allergies.

Offering a balanced diet is important as most of the vitamins and minerals that children need are covered by the four main food groups (except for vitamin D, see page 60):

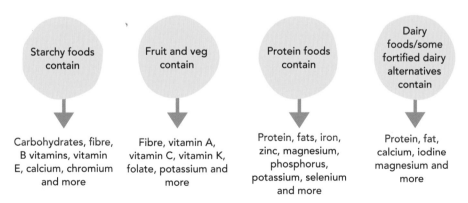

Starchy foods contain	Fruit and veg contain	Protein foods contain	Dairy foods/some fortified dairy alternatives contain
Carbohydrates, fibre, B vitamins, vitamin E, calcium, chromium and more	Fibre, vitamin A, vitamin C, vitamin K, folate, potassium and more	Protein, fats, iron, zinc, magnesium, phosphorus, potassium, selenium and more	Protein, fat, calcium, iodine magnesium and more

How Much Should My Toddler Be Eating?

Portion sizes for babies and toddlers are always a tricky topic. On the one hand, some parents prefer and benefit from having a clear or structured guide when it comes to feeding toddlers – which can help with confidence. However, on the other hand, research tends to show that young children, especially in the early years, are really good at regulating their own appetites. If we offer them a structured feeding routine and a nutrient-rich and varied diet, they are likely to regulate their intake pretty well.

In addition, every toddler will have their own energy and nutrient needs. Some children will need to eat more while other children will simply eat less, and that's OK. Day to day, meal to meal and even (especially in my experience with Raffy) week to week, the amount your little one eats is likely to fluctuate, depending on a number of factors – from how tired they are to whether they are growing, are unwell or are teething.

It's therefore important to respect our children's appetite cues and allow them some autonomy when it comes to *how much* they want to eat at mealtimes. This is known as 'responsive feeding'.

RESPONSIVE FEEDING

As we saw in the last chapter (page 34), responsive feeding is about helping your child to understand their own appetite and eat with autonomy, following their own hunger and fullness signals. If we encourage them to eat more or less of a meal, we may inadvertently override their body's own signals and therefore make them less 'responsive' to their own appetites over time.

Responsive feeding...

1. Sets up a mealtime structure for a child that is predictable and appropriate for their age/stage and offers a range of balanced food options, not over-restricting or cutting out any foods unnecessarily.

2. Ensures that mealtimes are pressure-free, engaging and nurturing.

3. Looks and listens out for signs that toddlers want more or less at mealtimes (see opposite) and responds appropriately, for example, by offering more if it's available or stopping the mealtime when they've shown they've had enough.

4. Gets to know the child's eating patterns and responds in a predictable way each time so that the child learns that there is always the same response to their own cues/reactions at mealtimes.

This results in the toddler learning to listen to their own signals when it comes to eating. If you're worried about how much your toddler is eating, get their weight and length/height checked. Ask a health visitor to explain their growth chart so you understand how their pattern of growth should track.

SIGNS YOUR TODDLER MAY WANT MORE FOOD

▼

Asking for more

Opening their mouth for more food

Crying when you take the plate away

Pointing to food

Reaching out for or grabbing food

Hanger!

SIGNS THEY MAY WANT TO STOP THE MEAL

▼

Crying during the meal

Asking to stop or saying 'no'

Clamping their mouth shut

Pushing the plate or spoon away

Getting distracted during the mealtime

Wanting to get down and play

Throwing food

My Step-by-Step Guide to Getting Portions Right

As parents, we often worry that we're not giving our children enough to eat, while at the same time being mindful of not wanting to feed them too much. It can seem like such a fine balance and causes a lot of anxiety for parents. My step-by-step guide should help you to get it just right:

1. Role model eating a balanced and varied diet. Also emphasise your own signs of fullness and hunger: 'I'm feeling hungry now', 'Oh, my tummy is a little full now; I'm going to stop.'

2. Offer the balanced diet we've described previously, with plenty of variety, to give your little one the right foundations and offer them just what they need to grow and thrive.

3. Offer a predictable structure to their food routine so they know when to expect meals and can build up an appetite for mealtimes.

4. Encourage two-way communication at mealtimes around their hunger and fullness feelings – 'What does it feel like when you're hungry?', 'Is your tummy feeling full?', 'Have you had enough?' – rather than you deciding when they've had enough.

5. Look out for and respond to their cues and signals that they've had enough and allow them to eat to appetite at meals. Offer seconds if they would like more. Try to respond in a predictable way each time.

6. Look at intakes over a week, not just in a single meal, as children's appetites can vary so much.

Over the next few pages you'll find a guide to serving sizes for toddlers. Use these ranges as a guide to how much to serve or plate up in the first instance, but let your toddler decide how much of anything they actually eat.

Serving size guide for toddlers

STARCHY FOODS: AROUND 5 SERVINGS A DAY

Couscous (cooked)
2–4 tbsp

Pasta (cooked)
2–5 tbsp

Bread
½–1 slice

Breadsticks
1–3

Oatcakes/
crackers
1–2

Rice (cooked)
2–5 tbsp

Cereal
3–6 tbsp

Pitta bread
¼–½

Chapatti
½–1

Potato
(medium-
sized, baked)
¼–½

Porridge
5–8 tbsp

Pancake
½–1

FRUIT AND VEG: 5 OR MORE SERVINGS A DAY

Broccoli (cooked)
½–2 tbsp or
1–4 small florets

Frozen mixed veg
(cooked) ½–2 tbsp

Carrot
1–3 tbsp or
2–6 sticks

Dried fruit
1–3 pieces
(large) or
½–2 tbsp
(small)

Banana
¼–1

Berries/
grapes
3–10

Avocado
½–2 tbsp

Cherry
tomatoes
1–3

Tinned fruits
2–4 tbsp

Frozen peas
(cooked)
½–2 tbsp

Tangerine
½–1 fruit

Spinach
½–2 tbsp

DAIRY FOODS: ABOUT 3 SERVINGS A DAY

Cheese sauce
1–3 tbsp

Cheese (processed)
1 ball

Yoghurt
3 tbsp or
125ml pot

Cheese (e.g.
cheddar)
2–4 tbsp/
20g

Low-sugar
custard
5–7 tbsp

Cottage
cheese
½–1 tbsp

Rice
pudding
2–4 tbsp

Yoghurt
alternative
120ml pot

Milk
100–120ml

PROTEIN/IRON: 2–3 SERVINGS A DAY

White fish
¼–1 small fillet or
1–2 fish fingers   ½–1 ½ tbsp tinned

Meat slice
(e.g. beef/
chicken)
1–2 small
slices

Beans
(cooked)
2–4 tbsp

Hummus
1–2 tbsp

Mince
(cooked)
2–4 tbsp

Eggs
(boiled)
½–1

Oily fish
¼–1 small
fillet or
½–1½ tbsp
tinned

Quorn/
tofu/soya
pieces
~50g

Falafel
1–3

Lentils
2–4 tbsp

Ground nuts/seeds
1–2 tbsp

Do Toddlers Need Snacks?

When it comes to snacks, the line from the government and other health bodies in the UK is that children under one don't need snacks, but over one it's recommended that they are included in a mealtime structure similar to three meals and two snacks every day. This is to make sure that children get all the energy and nutrients they need each day from food as they have small tummies and sometimes small appetites.

However, as ever, this is just blanket advice for everyone, not advice tailored to your little one. Although some children may well need snacks to top them up in between meals, and to help them meet their energy and nutrient needs, other children may not, and you might find that actually having snacks leads to them being slightly picky at mealtimes.

Does your child need snacks?

 Does your child seem hungry between meals? For example, are they unsettled, asking for foods or saying they are hungry regularly?

 Are they often over-hungry when it comes to mealtimes? For example, are they screaming for the food to be served?

 If offering snacks, do you think it's impacting on how much they eat at main meals? For example, do they show a lack of interest in the food offered at dinner?

 Are they growing and developing well?

Chat to your healthcare professional if you're worried about your child's weight or that they aren't getting enough nutrients. Weight and height measures can be a good indicator of toddlers getting enough calories.

WHAT TO OFFER

If you think snacks might be necessary to top up your little one, there are a few things to try to put into place:

- Stick to a routine around offering snacks rather than allowing your child to graze at random.

- Think 'mini meals' and offer a small portion.

- Try to balance snacks so your toddler has a chance to get foods from at least two or three of the main food groups at snack times.

The types of snacks that we tend to offer as parents are often easy, on-the-go, mess-free options that our kids love, such as shop-bought baby biscuits, crisps or fruity bars. In all honesty, sometimes these are fine, but often they can also be less nutrient-rich options. Remember that kids have small tummies and high energy and nutrient needs, so we need to make the most of their snacks too, as much as possible, which is why – ideally – snacks should be balanced.

Let's take a baby crisp, such as a carrot veggie puff, for example (see opposite). A typical baby crisp might offer some carbohydrates, a tiny amount of fibre and a tiny amount of protein. Whereas a baby crisp with chickpea dip and red pepper fingers can offer so much more, including exposure to different textures, colours and flavours. Toddlers will not get all the nutrients they need from eating these foods in small amounts, but adding them into a snack will contribute to their overall intake.

TIP: ADD IN A FEW EXTRAS

Think 'nutrients'. See if you can find little ways to add extras in at snack times too. For example, roll avocado in ground almonds, grate some cheese on top or offer hummus, nut butter or yoghurt as a dip on the side.

A TYPICAL BABY CRISP MIGHT OFFER:

Some carbohydrates

A tiny amount of protein

A tiny amount of fibre

WHEREAS A BABY CRISP + CHICKPEA DIP + RED PEPPER FINGERS OFFER:

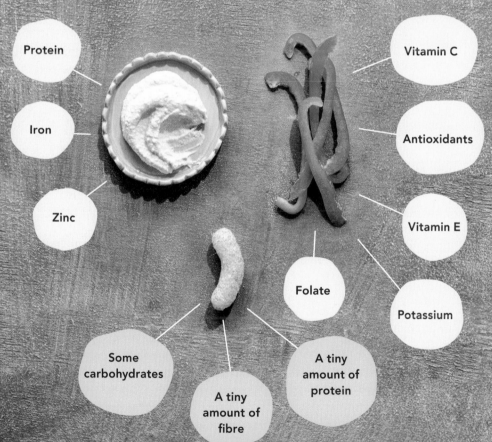

Protein

Iron

Zinc

Vitamin C

Antioxidants

Vitamin E

Potassium

Folate

Some carbohydrates

A tiny amount of fibre

A tiny amount of protein

SNACK BUILDER

Combine foods from two or three of the food groups at snack times to help top up nutrients and tick off those food groups. Remember to serve them as mini meals… So, here's how to do it:

1. Take a veg or fruit
+
2. Add a protein-/iron-rich food (or some dairy)
+
3. Add a carb

Here are some of my favourite balanced snack ideas for toddlers to give you some inspiration:

Oats with yoghurt and fruit

Egg with veg sticks and bread fingers

Veggie flapjacks

Crackers with nut butter and strawberries

Cheese and avocado with half an English muffin

Pancake strips with yoghurt and banana

Salmon and cucumber sandwich quarter

Savoury muffins

Energy balls

Milk, breadsticks and cucumber fingers

Mini wrap with chicken and avocado

Falafel bites with red pepper

Scones with some chopped strawberries and cheese/ yoghurt

Oatcakes with hummus and quartered grapes

Green beans and potato wedges with hummus dip

Breaded tofu sticks with fruit slices

Peanut butter with mashed banana and bread/crackers

Sweet potato wedges with yoghurt dip and paprika

Mini pot of peas with some fish fingers

Drinks for Toddlers

When it comes to drinks for toddlers, it's actually pretty simple: water is best for hydration for kids and that, along with milk, is all they need as fluids in the first years of their life, ideally!

There are lots of options out there, including 'baby juices' and squashes designed for babies and young children. However, there's no need to offer these and, in fact, they aren't really recommended either.

The trouble with offering drinks other than water is that:

- Your little one may enjoy the sweeter flavours and therefore start to refuse the plainer taste of water or milk.

- They may include free sugars and are very easy to drink in large amounts.

- They may include artificial sweeteners (see page 83).

- They can be quite acidic, which isn't good for tiny teeth as acid can damage the tooth enamel.

This is relevant for all drink options other than plain milk and water, and includes juice, fruit juice, juice drinks, squash, soft drinks, fizzy drinks and smoothies.

If you do offer juice options or smoothies, it's best to go for 100 per cent juice and dilute with water to reduce the amount of sugar that your toddler will consume in one go. It's recommended to dilute one part juice with ten parts water for under-fives.

It's OK to offer smoothies to young children every now and then, but they often contain high levels of blended fruits and therefore lots of freely available (blended) fruit sugars. You could try to reduce the sweetness of the smoothie and increase the variety it offers as well as reducing the sugar content by adding veggies along with the fruit or mixing it with yoghurt, oats, seeds and nut butters, for example. Offering the smoothie in a bowl with a spoon may also help to lessen the impact of the sugars on your child's teeth.

HOW MUCH TO OFFER?

The estimated amount of fluids (including milk and alternatives) that toddlers need is:

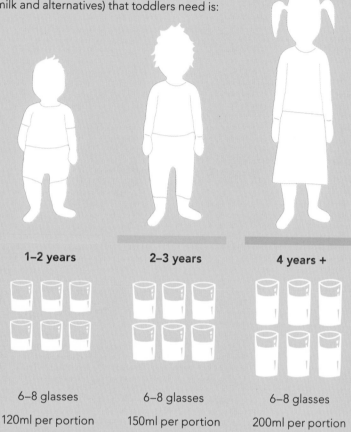

1–2 years	2–3 years	4 years +
6–8 glasses	6–8 glasses	6–8 glasses
120ml per portion	150ml per portion	200ml per portion

Try to make water available throughout the day. If your toddler is very active or the weather is hot they might need topping up a bit more. They may not be very good at communicating thirst, so having specific times in the day when they hydrate (for example, at meals and snack times) can be helpful reminders.

Remember that food also provides fluid to your toddler, especially if they eat plenty of fruits and vegetables. The fluid from food usually accounts for 20–30 per cent of kids' fluid requirements and the rest therefore needs to come from drinks, as shown above.

It might seem a little boring to only offer water, but ultimately your little one needs fluids to hydrate them, not to top up their energy levels or offer them sugar and sweetness.

CUPS AND BEAKERS

For children over one year of age, it's recommended to offer your toddler drinks in an open or free-flowing cup or beaker. 'Free-flowing' means that water will drip or spill out of the cup when it's turned upside down. These cups are better for your child's normal oral motor development and will help them learn to eventually master sipping without all the spills.

Strawed cups can also be helpful for when you're out and about with your toddler. Try to choose those with a lid, but without valves (which prevent spillage), and with a short, firm (and ideally weighted) straw if possible.

If your little one needs some encouragement to drink from an open cup, try:

- Letting them choose their 'big girl/boy cup' themselves.
- Using older role models and showing your toddler how they drink from and use open cups.
- Role modelling yourself, even using their cups to drink from too.
- Physically supporting them in using their new cups if they aren't familiar at first!
- Being consistent with your approach as much as you can.

THE LOWDOWN ON MILK

Both water and milk should be the main sources of fluid and hydration for toddlers. When it comes to milk, there are many options available:

Breast milk

Many toddlers will still be having breast milk as a main drink. It's hard to tell how much children get from the breast as you can't see a physical amount unless you're expressing. However, continue to breastfeed responsively and just try to make sure your little one isn't filling up on milk in place of food. You might need to juggle the routine around a bit if you're worried your toddler isn't eating enough at mealtimes. Speak to a health visitor if you have any questions about this.

If your toddler is breastfeeding around three or more times a day and having other dairy sources, such as cheese, yoghurt, milk in cereal or fortified non-dairy alternatives in their diet, you most likely won't need to offer them cow's milk as a drink. You can continue to breastfeed as long as you and your toddler both would like to.

Formula milk

Formula isn't really needed for children over one year of age, as they should be able to get most of their nutrients from food. Instead of formula, you can switch to full-fat cow's milk as a main drink alongside water from one year of age and throughout the toddler years. Some children, for example if they have allergies or are on specialised or prescribed formula, may need to continue having it. Check with your healthcare professional if you aren't sure.

Toddler 'growing up' milks

Toddler formula milks – often called 'growing up' milks – are not usually necessary for toddlers and there is no need to move from infant formula milk to toddler formula milk after one year of age. Switching to full-fat cow's milk will be sufficient for most toddlers, unless advised otherwise by a healthcare professional.

Dairy milk

The recommendation for dairy is to offer around three portions or 350–400ml of full-fat cow's milk for children aged one to four each day. This will count towards their fluid intake, so if your toddler is having 120ml of milk three times a day, this will contribute to three out of their six to eight glasses of fluid (see page 77).

Full-fat cow's milk is recommended for toddlers because they need the extra fat and calories this milk provides. However, once children get to two years of age, and as long as they are eating a well-balanced diet, they can switch to semi-skimmed milk. Skimmed milk isn't recommended as a drink until children are at least five years of age. Goat's and sheep's milk (full-fat versions) are also fine to offer as drinks from one year of age, as long as they are pasteurised.

However, when toddlers drink too much milk it can disrupt the balance of food in their diet and increase the risk of iron deficiency. It's often common for children who are a little choosy at mealtimes to fill up on milk in between meals and have little hunger when it comes to food.

Plant-based alternatives

Other plant-based alternatives, including soya, oat, almond, pea and coconut milk, are all fine to offer as drinks (or in foods) to toddlers as part of a healthy, balanced diet. However, it's best to opt for ones that are plain (not sweetened or flavoured) and fortified with nutrients, ideally including calcium, B vitamins and iodine, as they are not quite the same nutritionally as cow's milk. If your child has an allergy, it's best to discuss alternatives with your healthcare professional as they may need to take into account your little one's diet and any existing allergies before recommending a suitable alternative. Rice milk isn't recommended as a drink for toddlers until they are at least five years of age as it can contain small traces of arsenic.

Salt

Though research into how much salt kids should have in their diets and the impact of large intakes in the early years is limited, we do know that in adults high salt intake isn't a good idea and can lead to high blood pressure, which is a contributing factor to cardiovascular disease. Therefore, general recommendations are not to offer salty foods or added salt to toddlers' meals. They really don't need it and we ideally don't want them to develop a preference for salty foods later in life.

Most of us need to be cutting down on salt intake as a population, and this means helping children to enjoy the taste of foods without the need for seasoning with salt.

I have included a list of salt dos and don'ts opposite to help you, but remember it's all about balance, context and what happens over time, not at one meal or on one individual day.

AGE GROUP	MAXIMUM SALT INTAKE PER DAY (g)
0–6 months	< 1
6–12 months	1
1–3 years	2
4–6 years	3
7–10 years	5
11 years and above	6

DO

Try to balance meals – if they've had 'salty options' at some meals, then avoid salty options at others.

Limit the portions of salty foods such as some breads, cheese and condiments.

Offer a variety of foods to your toddler, for example, different types of carbohydrate, not just bread.

Try to make meals at home as much as possible, without salt. Use herbs and spices to flavour foods instead of salt.

Check labels and compare the salt content of packaged foods.

Limit salty foods such as sauces, foods tinned in salty water (brine) and smoked foods.

Share meals with your toddler and add any salt only to your portion at the end, if necessary.

Look at salt intakes over the whole day, not in a single meal.

DON'T

Add salt to your toddler's food – it's really not necessary.

Offer adult ready meals or highly processed foods to toddlers.

Be overly anxious about salt intakes; if they have a little that's OK.

Completely disregard nutrient-rich foods such as cheese, bread and some fish because they contain added salt.

Sugar

Sugar is such a big and confusing topic, especially for parents who are trying to navigate how much to offer, where it's coming from and what the problem is with it in the first place, while reading contradictory information online and seeing our kids seriously enjoy themselves when they do have some. Ultimately, it's recommended to limit the amount of sugar that children have in their diet. This is mainly because:

- Sugar contains energy, but very little else in the way of nutrition (and, remember, toddlers have tiny tummies and need nutrient- and energy-rich foods).

- Sugary foods are highly palatable, so it's easy for kids to eat more than they need.

- If eating lots of calories from sugars, it's likely that these could displace other nutrient-rich foods in children's diets.

- Sugar is simply not necessary – children can get all the nutrients and energy they need from other foods.

- Sugar can cause tooth decay.

WHAT COUNTS?

In the UK we tend to talk about added or 'free' sugars as being the sugars that we need to limit in adults' and children's diets, but what does this mean?

FREE SUGARS	NATURAL SUGARS
The sugars we should be mindful of are:	The sugars we don't need to worry about are:
• Sugars added at home or during cooking or processing.	• Naturally present in whole fresh fruits and vegetables (including dried, frozen and tinned fruits without added syrups).
• All added sugars including honey, maple syrup and coconut syrup.	• Naturally present in dairy products (for example, lactose and galactose).
• Sugars naturally present in fruit and veg once they are blended, juiced or puréed, for example fruit juice concentrates added to kids' food.	• Found within cereal and grains such as rice, pasta and flour.

Artificial Sweeteners

EU regulations state that sweeteners should not be used in foods prepared for infants and young children. This is mainly due to lack of data on the safety of sweeteners for infants and young children, as well as the fact that children need high-energy and nutrient-rich foods. Don't worry if you've already given your toddler foods containing artificial sweeteners – just try to avoid them in your little one's diet as much as possible.

HOW MUCH?

There isn't an official recommendation on how much sugar children under four should have in their diets. The government guidelines say to 'avoid sugar-sweetened drinks and food with sugar added to it' for children under the age of four. This would be ideal, but for many of us avoiding added sugars altogether is often not realistic or practical.

It's a good idea to think about how you can limit the amount of added or free sugar in your toddler's diet day to day, without overly restricting it and them being aware of this. Sugar and sugary foods are highly palatable and we're all born with a preference for sweet foods, so it's easy to see how children can end up eating more than needed. However, it's best not to offer lots of sweet foods to your toddler as this may encourage more of a preference for sweeter options, rather than enjoyment of a wide variety of flavours.

- Avoid offering your little one sugary foods and foods with added sugar before they're aware of them.
- Don't overly (or overtly) restrict them – allow your toddler to eat them when they are obviously available.
- Check labels when shopping and try to limit options that have added sugars for young children.
- Try to focus on small portions of sweet foods so that they don't affect your little one's appetite for the other meals or snacks they have that day.
- Avoid telling your child off or talking about how 'bad' sugar is.

It's OK for your little one to have small amounts of added sugars in their diet – think about their intakes over a whole week rather than on a single day.

Developing eating skills

With any luck, your toddler will be fairly competent with a wide
variety of textures and with self-feeding and using finger foods by
now, and most of their foods will only need slight modifications.
However, if you don't feel your toddler is quite there yet, try not to
worry – children's eating skills are still developing after one year of
age, and they all reach developmental milestones at different paces.
They still have plenty of time to practise, hone and master those
skills, and a lot of that will come with role modelling and being
offered practice with a variety of textures over time.

Right up until around four or five years of age, your toddler might
still be mastering and developing eating skills and learning exactly
how to manipulate different textures in their mouth, so you still might
need to adapt some foods for them.

Some children may be able to cope more easily with different
textures and shapes of foods as their feeding skills develop and
mature. Therefore, being responsive to your child's eating and
feeding skills is key – watch and learn, but remember that some
foods pose more of a risk of choking and may need to be avoided or
modified (see opposite).

Squash, chop or mash things if you're worried at all, but do make
sure you still offer your toddler plenty of textures in their daily diet.
They need to be offered a variety of textures at this stage and
practise self-feeding in order to help them to develop mature eating
skills and be confident with eating a varied diet with similar textures
to adults.

CHOKING HAZARDS

Young children can choke on any food, and as such I always recommend that parents do some basic baby/toddler first aid training. Two key factors put younger children at greater risk of choking than older children and adults:

1. Their small airway size.

2. Their less mature eating skills.

Both of these will grow and mature with your child's age and development, especially if you offer a variety of textures.

There are some foods that pose more of a risk of choking than others, and will need to be adapted or avoided until your child is older (generally four or five years of age). This is not an exhaustive list and the advice varies around the world, but it's good to remember a few principles and simply alter foods you don't feel comfortable with offering (while being mindful of ensuring plenty of texture in your toddler's foods).

RISKIER FOODS	SUCH AS	HOW TO PREP THEM
Are hard and break off in chunks	Raw carrot, raw apple or sticks of cheese	Grate, thinly slice or cook before offering
Are hard and round when whole	Whole nuts, peanuts, boiled or chewy sweets, popcorn, mini chocolate eggs	Offer nuts and peanuts as ground nuts or as thin nut butter; avoid sweets, popcorn and mini chocolate eggs, ideally
Are round and squidgy with soft edges	Whole grapes, large blueberries, olives, cherry tomatoes, large beans, chickpeas and sausages	Quarter these foods lengthways, squash them flat (blueberries) or mash them slightly with the back of a fork (beans/chickpeas)
Are hard to chew	Tough meats, stringy foods, tough skins, and those foods that have chewy or sticky textures like toffees and marshmallows	Shred large chunks of meat or offer as mince, cut stringy bits off foods and avoid super-sticky/chewy sweets
Are slippery	Some tinned fruits and hard jelly cubes	Avoid jelly cubes and serve tinned fruits chopped up with yoghurt or coat with milled seeds, for example

As well as the points above, there are some things you can do from a safety perspective to minimise the risk of your toddler choking:

 Always feed them when sitting upright, ideally in a highchair or chair where they are fully supported, and avoid allowing them to walk around while eating.

Avoid feeding toddlers in car seats or prams as choking incidences can increase when doing this.

Always sit with your child when they are eating and avoid wandering off after meals are served.

Keep mealtimes calm, give your little one plenty of time to eat and allow them to feed themselves.

Foods to avoid

Aside from some of the potential choking hazards (and salty or sugary foods), there really aren't many other foods that toddlers need to 'avoid' in their diets. However, as children are considered to be a vulnerable group, due to their developing immune systems, it's generally considered that the following foods need to be avoided or limited for children until they are around four or five years of age.

AVOID	LIMIT
Unpasteurised dairy, including cheese made from unpasteurised milk, due to the risk of listeria. It's fine if you cook these first. Try to check labels on dairy foods to make sure they are made using pasteurised milk.	Some cheeses: for example, avoid mould-ripened soft cheeses and soft blue-veined cheeses as there is a risk of listeria. They're fine to offer if you cook these first.
Undercooked or raw eggs, unless they have the Red Lion stamp on them. If eggs don't have the Red Lion stamp, it's best to cook them all the way through for toddlers to decrease any risk of salmonella.	Certain types of fish: Boys from 0–16 years old are recommended to have no more than 4 portions of oily fish a week. Girls from 0–16 years old are recommended to have no more than 2 portions of oily fish a week, as these fish can contain mercury and other PCBs, which can build up in the body over time and may harm future pregnancies.
Rice milk as a drink – this can contain trace amounts of arsenic and, as young children can drink fairly large amounts of milk, it's best to avoid offering rice milk.	
Raw meat, fish or shellfish – due to the potential risk of food poisoning.	
Shark, swordfish or marlin – these big fish can build up high levels of mercury, which is dangerous for developing young children.	

Meal Planner

Here's a sample meal planner to help your child meet their nutritional requirements throughout the week. I have balanced out food groups

	MONDAY	TUESDAY	WEDNESDAY
Breakfast Around 7am	Plain yoghurt with oats, nut butter and banana slices	Fortified low-sugar cereal with milk, chopped dried fruits and milled seeds	Porridge with grated carrot, milled seeds and yoghurt
Snack Around 10am	Raspberry chia seed jam on toast with milk	Boiled egg with kiwi slices and toast strips	Veggie sticks with dip
Lunch Around 12.30pm	Fishy pasta in a cream cheese and avocado sauce	Orzo in a veggie lentil tomato sauce with cheese	Veggie-packed quesadillas with beans and cheese
Dinner Around 4pm	Lentil/chicken chilli with veggies and rice	Beef/chickpea stew with veg, yoghurt and rice	Spaghetti with chicken/tofu chunks in a veg sauce with cheese
Optional extra snack ideas	Sweet potato wedges with dip	Yoghurt with milled seeds	Pitta triangles, cream cheese and carrot

very carefully and I have deliberately made the meals a bit vague to allow for individuality. Check out the recipes in this book in case you need some inspiration! You can find even more recipes on my website (srnutrition.co.uk) and in my first book, *How to Wean Your Baby*.

THURSDAY	FRIDAY	SATURDAY	SUNDAY
Scrambled egg on wholegrain toast with chopped pepper	Pancakes with plain yoghurt and berries	Fortified low-sugar cereal with milk, fruit and milled seeds	Porridge with grated apple and nut butter
Yoghurt, fruit and mini breadsticks	Mini tortilla wrap with hummus, cheese and veggies	Oatcake with spread and berries	Cheese and crackers with veg sticks
Pitta bread served with a bean and veggie stew topped with cheese	Wholemeal toast with hummus and veggie fingers	Cheese and veg omelette with potato wedges	Pasta with tuna and sweetcorn in a yoghurt sauce
Jacket potato with beans and side salad with cheese	Easy Eggy Veggie Potatoes with cheese	Baked salmon with mash and veggies and a dollop of yoghurt	Chickpea and couscous salad
Toast and spread with fruit	Flapjack fingers with dip	Chicken, yoghurt, red pepper sticks	Boiled egg and pear

FEEDING OUT AND ABOUT

3

The reality is that there are going to be multiple times when children will need to be fed out of the home or away from us. This can cause concern for many parents, who are perhaps used to being the one feeding their toddler and who like to know what they are eating. However, eating out and about can be great for little ones – new experiences, new tastes, new flavours and new people to watch and learn from. Eating out with toddlers doesn't have to be stressful!

Eating on the Go

There are so many food and snack options available for toddlers that sometimes it can be a bit of a minefield for us to work out which options we feel comfortable with. Of course, ultimately it's best to offer children home-cooked foods as much as possible, so we can:

- Feel more in control of exactly what they are eating.
- Be confident about the ingredients they're eating.
- Get them familiar with the flavours of our own cooking.
- Easily vary the textures.
- Offer a wider variety of foods.
- Add extra nutrients to top-up intakes.
- Offer similar foods to the rest of the family.

However, I know from my own experience that this isn't always possible and convenient, and easy options can be great for busy parents when in a rush, on the go or out and about.

Some of the commercially available options for young toddlers aren't ideal, so you may need to be a little savvy with the choices you make.

BE SAVVY WITH SUPERMARKET SNACKS

Often they aren't very rich in nutrients – baby crisps, for example. This means that little ones can fill up on them, but without getting the balance of nutrients that they need.

Sometimes these foods can contain added sugar and salt – like some fruity bars or baby biscuits – which really isn't necessary or ideal for young children (see pages 80–83).

Sometimes these foods are very sweet to appeal to young children and might contain lots of 'free sugars' (see page 82) – processed fruit bars or chewy fruit roll-ups, for example. These aren't great options for tiny teeth.

Quite often these foods don't offer 'balanced' options, which is what we want to be looking for in toddlers' meals and snacks.

WHAT CAN WE DO?

Don't worry too much – having foods such as baby crisps or fruity bars every now and then won't do your toddler any harm. It's more important that they don't have them regularly in their diet.

However, try not to make these their main source of meals and/or snacks and try to keep them to occasional, convenient options.

Think of ways you can offer smaller portions of these foods and bulk them out with other food groups, for example a sprinkle of milled seeds on top, a plain yoghurt to dip a fruity bar in or some veggie sticks along with some baby crisps (see page 73).

Choose options that have no added salt and sugar and remember that fruit juices, fruit juice concentrates and fruit powders added to snacks still count as 'free sugars'.

Lastly, have a quick check of the nutrition panels – my step-by-step guide on the next page should help!

LABEL READING

Learning to read labels efficiently sounds like a daunting task, but it can actually be pretty simple when you know what to look for.

A guide to reading food labels

1. Check the nutritional information panel on the back of the packet (see the next page for a guide to reading these).

2. Use the 'Per 100g' column on the nutritional information panel to check the levels of salt (sodium), sugar and saturated fat, and try to choose foods that are low in these nutrients. Below is a guide you can check to see if the levels are considered high, medium or low. Remember that the amount of food eaten matters and will determine how much salt, saturated fat and sugar your toddler actually takes in. Also, just because something is 'high' doesn't mean that the food is 'bad' – it's simply high in that nutrient. That's where the ingredients list can come in handy...

3. Check the ingredients list. On the next page you can find tips on picking these apart as they can be confusing. The ingredients panel will tell you where the nutrients are actually coming from; for example, are the sugars coming from whole pieces of fruit or from free sugars, such as honey or sucrose?

Practise reading these labels, but remember that what really matters is moderation, balance and some role modelling from you, not what your little one is eating at one meal or snack time.

	SUGAR	FAT	SATURATES	SALT
What is high?	OVER 15g	OVER 20g	OVER 5g	OVER 1.5g
What is medium?	BETWEEN 5g AND 15g	BETWEEN 3g AND 20g	BETWEEN 1.5g AND 5g	BETWEEN 0.3g AND 1.5g
What is low?	5g AND BELOW	3g AND BELOW	1.5g AND BELOW	0.3g AND BELOW

Serving size: manufacturer's suggestion for what's a portion. Check what's recommended but note that adult products will have portion sizes only relevant to adults.

Nutrients: legally, nutrients need to be listed in the order shown here. If the nutrients or vitamins have been added, they will be shown at the bottom. So if you see 'iron' or 'iodine' here it's likely they've been added.

NUTRITIONAL INFORMATION

Servings per package – 5.5

Serving size – 30g (2/3 cups)

	Per serving	Per 100g
Energy	432kj/103kcal	1441kj/344kcal
Protein	2.8g	9.39g
Fat		
Total	0.4g	1.2g
Saturated	0.1g	0.3g
Carbohydrate		
Total	18.9g	62.9g
Sugars	3.5g	11.8g
Fibre	6.6g	21.2g
Sodium	65mg	215mg

Per serving: shows the nutrients in the product as per the serving size they recommend. This is how much of the nutrients your child will get if they eat a 'portion' of the product.

Calories: shows the energy gained per serving or 100g of the product. We measure this in kilojoules (kj) and calories (kcal). There is no need to count calories but look out for food that is nutrient-rich, rather than just high in calories.

Carbohydrate: shows the types of carbs in the food, including sugar and fibre.

There are lots of names for **sugar** – fruit juice, fruit juice concentrate, syrups (agave, date), coconut blossom nectar, honey, molasses, and lots of ingredients ending in 'ose', such as glucose, fructose and dextrose. These count as added or free sugars.

INGREDIENTS

Rice, Sugar, Glucose Syrup, Fat Reduced Cocoa Powder, Salt, Cocoa Mass, **Barley** Malt Extract, Flavourings

Ingredients are listed in order of size. The first ingredient makes up the most of the product.

Allergens will always be shown in bold.

Salt is sometimes referred to as 'sodium' and will read a lower amount than it would if it were listed as salt (sodium is just part of the salt molecule).

Lunch Boxes

When it comes to packing lunch boxes, it really comes back to balance and ensuring that your toddler has an opportunity to get plenty of energy and nutrients via a balance of food groups (see Chapter 2). That means when you're packing a lunch box you need to think about offering:

✓ Some starchy carbs, such as bread, potatoes, pasta and wraps;

✓ Some veg and/or fruits;

✓ Some protein- and iron-rich foods;

✓ Some dairy or alternatives;

✓ A drink: milk or water.

Here are my top tips on packing a healthy lunch and some fun lunch box ideas for you to try:

- Put a little note in to give them something else to be excited about when opening up their lunch box.

- Try to offer a nice variety in their lunches so they are less likely to get bored, especially if they are having packed lunches regularly.

- Let them have a choice in the contents of their lunch boxes and get them involved in making them. Spreading, chopping and packing their own lunch box might just make them a little more eager to eat what goes into it.

- Include something you know they love eating. This is likely to make them more willing to try the rest.

- If you're able to, try getting a jazzy lunch box, which might just help them to be more excited to show off their lunch.

- Include a toy, sticker or some fun spoons for them to use at lunchtimes to add some more interest.

- In hot weather, add a bottle of frozen water to keep the food cold throughout the day.

LUNCH BOX IDEAS

The graphic below shows some perfect food ideas to help you create a balanced lunch box for your toddler. The sections are split into the food groups and these are just examples of foods you could include for each food group.

Nursery Food

For many parents, when their little one goes off to nursery it's the first time that what they eat isn't completely within their control, and that can be quite daunting. All of a sudden you can feel a bit out of the loop – I know this feeling only too well!

The food on offer at nurseries is hugely variable. Some nurseries make the food themselves in their own kitchen, some follow a packed-lunch-only policy and some use outside catering companies – it varies all over the UK, so it's worth checking with your child's nursery before they start.

Added to this, although there are government guidelines, there are no *legal* requirements as to what nursery meals have to offer, and different nursery settings interpret the guidelines in different ways.

NURSERY FOOD GUIDELINES

The guidelines suggest that what toddlers should have at lunch should be similar to what is described in the graphic on the opposite page. Ideally, your toddler should be offered a 'balanced' meal when they are at nursery as well as healthy snacks and plenty of fluids.

In my experience, communication is so key when it comes to someone else feeding your child. If you ever have concerns or questions, don't be afraid to ask the staff. For example, you might want more information on:

- Whether you can have a copy of their menus so you know what's on offer week to week.

- What guidelines they follow around the food they offer.

- How food is served.

- What environment your toddler eats their meals in.

- If they have a policy around mealtimes or any food brought in.

- What they do about allergies or different dietary requirements.

- How they encourage children to drink water throughout the day.

- Feedback on your little one's eating day to day – this is helpful for you to know what and how much to serve later.

Also, feel free to ask questions about how they present food, what they do if food isn't eaten and whether food is used as a reward or punishment. The more this is spoken about and asked, the more nurseries might be likely to take on board feedback or appreciate different ways of approaching food practices with young children.

CURRENT UK NURSERY LUNCH GUIDELINES

1 X CARB FOOD
Offer white and wholegrain varieties ✓

AT LEAST 1 X FRUIT AND/OR VEG
Vary the type offered ✓

1 X PUDDING
Focus on milk-/fruit-based options
Offer a variety
Limit cakes and biscuits ✓

DRINKS
Offer fresh water and milk only ✓

1 X PROTEIN
Offer meat, fish and alternatives
1 x oily fish every three weeks ✓

DAIRY OR ALTERNATIVES
Offer 3 times a day, can be at lunch
Offer lower-sugar options ✓

WHAT TO EXPECT WHEN YOUR TODDLER STARTS NURSERY

NURSERY APPROACH	WHY DO THEY DO THIS?	HOW TO HANDLE IT
Different routines to your own	All children will have different routines and the nursery has to cater for multiple children in one go.	Sometimes you need to find a new routine on the days when your little one is in nursery and this is OK – simply stick to your own home structure on non-nursery days.
Offering regular snacks	Children at nursery will sometimes have 90 per cent of their food for the day at the setting. This means that there need to be opportunities for children to get enough calories and nutrients throughout the day.	Snacks are often the norm in nurseries, so you might just need to adjust what you're offering at home to compensate. For example, if the nursery offers a snack and a light tea from 3–5pm, you might find that your toddler isn't hungry for a full meal when they get home.
Puddings	'Puddings' can be helpful in a nursery setting as children have different preferences for foods. If children refuse their mains, puddings offer a chance to get some calories (and hopefully some nutrients) in when they are at nursery for quite a long day. Puddings may contain added sugars, though, but ideally should be based on milk or fruit/veg.	If your little one is young enough not to be aware of 'puddings', ask if they can have an alternative option (often they can have fruit or yoghurt instead). Have a conversation with the nursery to see if there is any scope for making changes if you aren't happy with the puddings on offer.

NURSERY APPROACH	WHY DO THEY DO THIS?	HOW TO HANDLE IT
Different practices to encourage children to eat – for example, 'one more spoon or no pudding'	Different nurseries will have different methods of handling food refusal as they cater for all appetites and needs.	Carry on role modelling and practising your own methods at home. Try having a chat to nursery staff about the approach you take and why.
Smaller portion sizes	Some children may have and want second helpings while others may leave a lot of food on their plates. It's hard to know how much overall food is needed when you're serving multiple children.	Ask for feedback on how much your child is eating and check that they don't seem to be feeling hungry at nursery. Encourage your toddler to eat to appetite as much as you can. You might need to offer extras at home on nursery days.
Offering less 'toddler-friendly' foods	This is one of the most common things I'm asked about, but try to remember that nurseries have to cater to all needs and have a duty of care to avoid children being hungry all day. They need to provide food that children will eat, which can make it difficult when catering to multiple tastes.	Ask to see what's on offer, as well as recipes and ingredients lists if possible so you can see the detail. Sometimes titles are misleading, for example 'corn cakes' might be a nutrient-dense option. Have a chat with the nursery if you're worried at all and let them know about guidelines on offer from the government.

Eating Out

I have to confess that eating out is one of my favourite things to do and I've never really let having kids stop me! Often parents worry about eating out with kids because of the lack of control over what goes into kids' foods, but also due to the environment, the chaos and the worries over toddlers not eating what's on offer. However, it can also be a fun social occasion and toddlers can have some new and exciting eating experiences when dining out too.

If you only eat out occasionally, you don't really need to worry too much about the food on the odd occasion of eating at a café or restaurant. Lots of places cater really well for children these days and are more than happy to accommodate requests. However, here are some things you can try to feel more confident in feeding your toddler out and about:

- Call ahead/check their website to see what's on offer or how they cater for toddlers.

- Try sharing part of your own meal along with some sides so they are getting plenty of variety.

- Ask the chef to hold the salt, sugar or chilli in dishes, where possible or ask to see information on what's in the meals.

- See new meals and new flavours as 'experimenting'.

- Think about offering a bigger meal at lunch if going out for dinner.

A few other helpful tips to make eating out more pleasant:

- Take bibs and plates/cups/cutlery with you.

- Take wipes, a bag and other bits for a mammoth clean-up after (it's nice to help a little), but also to wipe down the table or highchairs beforehand too.

- Take a small snack to offer while you wait. Crackers, oatcakes or some cooked veggies can offer a good distraction.

- Take table activities like colouring, books or stackable cups.

Don't stress too much over what's on offer if it's just an occasional event or you're having time together with your toddler or family. Making it enjoyable, offering a variety and avoiding any obvious pressure or restriction will be the most useful things to remember.

My Step-by-Step Guide to Helping Kids Love Their Food

Finally, here is my quick step-by-step guide to helping toddlers learn to love their food. It's a summary of everything I covered in the previous chapters. If you're short on time and just want a recap, read on!

1. Build the foundations

Offer a healthy, balanced diet and a regular meal schedule that focuses on safe and appropriate foods for your toddler's age and development (see Chapter 2).

2. Role model

Show your toddler how to eat well and how to *enjoy* the foods they eat by adopting a 'do as I do' not a 'do as I say' approach when feeding them. Eating meals together can be an important part of them learning about food.

3. Minimise mealtime pressures

Keep it light. Instead of encouraging toddlers to 'eat up' – by coaxing or bribing them to have more or try something new – try saying, 'That's OK, you don't have to eat it' and focus on feeding yourself.

4. Avoid negative food (and body) talk

Talk positively about all foods and avoid talking about foods as 'good' or 'bad' options or encouraging a food hierarchy, for example sweet foods = desirable 'treat' foods. Instead, help your little one to understand the importance of balance and variety by demonstrating what this is and how you do it yourself (see pages 24–25).

5. Bring food into other aspects of their lives

Take them shopping, involve them in dinner parties and picnics, have food toys or mini kitchens for them to play with, get them growing and cooking, bring food into messy play occasions or simply read to them about food and where it comes from as part of their general learning and development.

6. Offer them variety

Think of offering different foods, colours, textures, flavours, various meals and even the same food in multiple ways, such as carrot as a dip, boiled and roasted with herbs, mashed, grated and stirred into sauces, or mixed into pie toppings or in porridge. Even when times get tough and lots is refused, variety is shown over and over again to help kids enjoy a wider variety later in life, so keep going.

7. Keep going

Avoid taking foods out of your child's diet just because they've been refused a few times. Often a liking of new tastes is acquired over time and research shows that repeatedly offering foods builds familiarity and acceptance towards them. So don't eliminate single foods or whole food groups from the menu; keep offering, eating yourself and allowing your child to see, smell, touch and eventually taste these rejected items again.

8. No food fights

As much as you can, keep the environment around food/meals and snacks as calm and enjoyable as you can. Mealtime stress can have a knock-on effect on how your little one feels about food. Focus on making the mealtimes themselves enjoyable again before tackling exactly what's being eaten.

9. Follow their lead

Give your toddler the freedom to express and listen to their own appetite at mealtimes (rather than simply encouraging them to eat what you think they should). Sometimes this can be a tricky one to put into practice, but the more independence you give them around food choices and portion sizes, the more they will learn about eating well and following their own, natural appetites.

10. Expect ups and downs

It's so important to accept that there will be days when your little one doesn't eat much at all and other days when they eat plenty. Their journey with food isn't linear, so don't worry about bumps in the road and days and weeks of food refusal or being picky – it's part of the process of feeding kids and the earlier on you accept that, the more relaxed your feeding journey with them should be (see pages 35–47)!

RECIPES

4

I love food and so I wanted this part of the book to show how much food can mean to a family. These recipes are all perfect options for families *and* toddlers. Most of them have now become staples in my household and I'm just so happy I get to share them with you all.

When developing these recipes, I took feedback from my last book and blog and wanted to create even more simple, easy and accessible recipes. Here you'll find plenty of traybakes, snacks and versatile options to make your life easier.

It's so important for me to ensure my recipes can be adapted to suit any style of eating. Most of the recipes in this book can be made plant-based – wherever possible, I have included a 'can be easily adapted' symbol and provided suggestions in the introduction and ingredients to indicate how easy it is to make swaps, like substituting tofu, beans or pulses for meat, or leaving out the dairy and/or replacing it with non-dairy alternatives (see opposite).

I like to advocate that we don't need to make separate meals for kids and adults, and that everyone can share one meal that is balanced, delicious and colourful. That's what I've tried to create throughout this little recipe section here.

Some recipes might take a little longer, but I have created most of them with my two sprogs at my heels! I loved exploring these with my children, getting them to taste-test and help finalise the recipes with me – they were so central in the whole process of testing them out and I hope your little ones love them just as much as mine do!

A QUICK NOTE ON INGREDIENTS

Some of the recipes that follow call for a flaxseed or chia seed 'egg', which is really useful if you are avoiding eggs. To make either of these, mix 1 tablespoon of ground flaxseed/chia seeds with 3 tablespoons of warm water for every whole egg used in the recipes and leave to one side for 5 minutes to thicken. You can replace the flaxseed/chia seed egg with a free-range large egg or one mashed banana in many recipes too.

Dairy alternatives: it's always easy to swap dairy-free spreads for butter, and plain dairy-free alternatives for cheese and yoghurt. Any recipe that uses milk can be your milk of choice, whether that's dairy or plant milk.

Meat in many of the recipes can also be replaced with beans, lentils or tofu. I tested many of the recipes with plant-based meat alternatives and they worked just as well. If you're looking for more meat, you can also easily swap fish for tofu and chicken, beef, lamb or pork for lentils or beans. (Remember to adapt cooking times so the meat is thoroughly cooked.)

You can use shop-bought breadcrumbs, but it's so easy to make your own – simply blitz one to two slices of wholemeal bread (stale bread works perfectly) in a food processor or high-speed blender and use straight away or pop them in the freezer for when you need them.

RECIPE SYMBOLS

 Vegan

 Vegetarian

 Can be easily adapted

 No cooking required

 Can be frozen

Breakfast

Breakfast is definitely one of my children's favourite meals and always has been! I find it a great way to top up their intakes before we start the day. Luckily, both Raffy and Ada are usually pretty hungry in the morning so they tend to gobble up whatever's on offer. For this reason, I love to vary what they have at breakfast time.

Porridge is a favourite in our house and some of the low-sugar, fortified cereals are great for quick breakfasts too. There are plenty of really simple options out there, but in this section I offer a real variety of easy breakfasts you can make for your toddler, to give them a good balance of foods first thing in the day. Some of these recipes take a little longer to make and might be best for the weekends, but lots of them are simple options you can make the night before (or freeze for another day) and just pop out for a ready-made option in the morning!

CARROT CAKE RICE PUDDING

Prep: 5 minutes
Cook: 10 minutes
Serves: 4 toddlers

This super-tasty, quick rice pudding is a great alternative to traditional rice pudding, without the added sugars. It also includes some texture and veggies, which are always great for added variety. This recipe can be served hot or cold.

• •

250g pouch no added salt pre-cooked rice (sticky rice or long grain work well)
200ml milk of choice
1 medium carrot, peeled and finely grated
1 tsp ground cinnamon
20g raisins, finely chopped
1 ripe banana, peeled and mashed, to serve (optional)

1. Mix the rice, milk, carrot, cinnamon and raisins in a saucepan.

2. Cook for 8–10 minutes on a medium heat until the milk has evaporated and you have a nice thick pudding. Add an extra splash of milk if needed to loosen the mixture.

3. Serve warm or cold with the mashed banana mixed in at the end (if using). Make sure you cool any leftovers within 1 hour.

Leftovers can be transferred to an airtight container and stored in the fridge for 24 hours or frozen in individual portions and defrosted in the fridge overnight before using.

TODDLER-FRIENDLY GRANOLA

Prep: 5 minutes
Cook: 20–25 minutes
Makes: about 200g

My son loves granola, but shop-bought varieties can contain high levels of sugar and whole nuts, making them unsuitable for toddlers. This is one of my favourite recipes in this book! It's a super-simple granola, with no added sugar, and it tastes so delicious. It's also very versatile as it can be used as a basic granola with just milk, with yoghurt and berries, or sprinkled on top of pancakes, porridge or cereals. You can easily make this recipe vegan by using a plant-based yoghurt.

100g porridge oats
35g ground almonds
1 apple, cored and grated
juice and grated zest of 1 small orange
½ tsp ground cinnamon
yoghurt and mixed seasonal berries,
   chopped, to serve (optional)

1. Preheat the oven to 200°C/180°C fan. Line a baking tray with greaseproof paper.

2. Mix together the oats, ground almonds, apple and orange zest in a bowl. Squeeze over the orange juice, add the cinnamon and mix to combine.

3. Spread the mixture over the prepared baking tray and bake for 15 minutes. Give it a stir and bake for a further 5 minutes or so, until golden and crispy.

4. Take the granola out of the oven and leave to cool before transferring to an airtight container, where it can be stored for a few weeks.

5. If serving with yoghurt, sprinkle granola on top of yoghurt and top with some fresh berries.

 Sprinkle the granola on other brekkies, snacks and puddings to add some extra crunch, nutrients and flavour!

BLUEBERRY BAKED OATS

Prep: 10 minutes
Cook: 20 minutes
Serves: 4 toddlers and 2 adults

Oats are an absolute staple in our house! We have porridge on a regular basis and I love using oats in baking – as you'll see throughout this section. This recipe makes delicious flapjack-style baked oats that you can eat in slabs or serve warm with some yoghurt. It's also a fab one to help mix up breakfast times. It feels quite luxurious, but is so easy to make and your kids will love it, both warm and left to cool for eating out and about. I also love having this in the morning with the kids – it's definitely one for the adults too!

100g porridge oats
2 tbsp smooth peanut butter, plus extra to serve
2 tbsp milled seeds (sunflower, linseed or pumpkin work well)
1 ripe banana, peeled and mashed
100g fresh blueberries, roughly chopped, plus extra to serve
50ml milk of choice
1 chia seed egg (see page 109) or 1 large free-range egg, beaten

1. Preheat the oven to 200°C/180°C fan. Line a 20cm square ovenproof tin with greaseproof paper.

2. In a bowl, mix all the ingredients together, except the chia seed egg. Once combined, add the chia seed egg and mix well.

3. Tip the mixture into the prepared tin and spread it evenly to the sides. Bake for 20 minutes in the middle of the oven until cooked through and the blueberries are gooey.

4. Serve warm, divided into bowls with some extra chopped blueberries and a drizzle of peanut butter and/or a dollop of yoghurt on top.

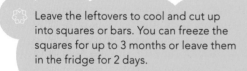

Leave the leftovers to cool and cut up into squares or bars. You can freeze the squares for up to 3 months or leave them in the fridge for 2 days.

PEAR BREAKFAST BITES

Prep: 10 minutes
Cook: 15–20 minutes
Makes: 18 bites

These are like mini muffins and can be eaten hot or cold. They are great for breakfasts or a mid-morning snack when out and about. They also freeze really well. This recipe isn't super sweet, but packs a lot of flavour and my kids love it. I hope these will go down a treat in your household like they do in ours.

dairy-free spread
    or oil, for greasing
415g tinned pears, drained (choose
    pears in juice, not syrup)
1 ripe banana, peeled
50ml milk of choice (or 50ml
    reserved pear juice)
1 flaxseed egg (see page 109) or
    1 large free-range egg, beaten
80g porridge oats
2 tsp ground cinnamon
175g self-raising flour

1. Preheat the oven to 200°C/180°C fan. Line a muffin tray with mini cases (18 in total) or grease the holes.

2. Roughly chop a large handful of the drained pears and keep to one side. Add the rest of the pears to a high-speed blender along with the banana and milk (or reserved pear juice, if using) and blend until smooth and well mixed.

3. Transfer the blended mixture to a bowl and add the flaxseed egg, oats and cinnamon and give it a good mix. Now add the flour and stir to combine.

4. Spoon the mixture into the cases and top each with some of the reserved pear chunks.

5. Bake for 15–20 minutes until golden and a skewer inserted into the centre of a muffin comes out clean.

6. Remove from the oven and lift the muffins from the tray onto a cooling rack. Leave to cool a little before serving. Once cool, pop in the freezer for when you need them or store in an airtight container for up to 3 days.

You can mix a little of the drained pear juice with some yoghurt to make a sweet pear yoghurt dip for the bites to be dipped in!

BEETROOT AND SALMON MUFFINS

Prep: 10–15 minutes
Cook: 15–20 minutes
Makes: 12 muffins

My family are big fans of breakfast muffins! They feel very continental, but the truth is that they are a super-easy breakfast option. Ada loves finger foods and I'm so time-limited now, so these muffin-style brekkies really work for us. They can be eaten cold, but sometimes I like to reheat them in the oven until they are hot all the way through, which usually takes 8–10 minutes. I also love to keep a few in the fridge and take them for an out-and-about brekkie the next day (or use them as part of the kids' lunches)!

212g tin salmon (MSC approved), drained
120g cheddar or red Leicester cheese, grated
2 balls (about 120g) vacuum-packed beetroot in natural juices, drained and grated
2 large free-range eggs, beaten, or 2 flaxseeds eggs (see page 109)
100ml milk of choice
2 spring onions, trimmed and finely chopped
50g unsalted butter or dairy-free spread, melted, plus extra for greasing
150g self-raising flour

1. Preheat the oven to 210°C/190°C fan. Line a 12-hole muffin tray with cases or grease the holes with a little butter or spread.

2. Put the salmon into a bowl and break it up with a fork. Add most of the cheese (saving a little for the top) and the beetroot to the bowl, along with the eggs and milk. Mix together, add the spring onions and melted butter and stir to combine.

3. Add the flour and mix until you have a thick batter.

4. Divide the batter between the muffin cases and top with the reserved cheese.

5. Cook for 15–20 minutes until golden and a skewer inserted in the middle of a muffin comes out clean. These muffins will keep in the fridge for 2 days or can be frozen for up to 3 months. You can defrost them overnight and serve cold or reheat until piping hot.

Use fish in foods like muffins to add some omega-3 and help your toddler get their oily fish portions for the week.

MINI BAKED EGGS SHAKSHUKA

V A ❄

Prep: 10 minutes
Cook: 15–20 minutes
Serves: 2 toddlers and 2 adults

This recipe takes a little longer to make but is great for a weekend brekkie option – you can also scale it up to make a bigger batch in a saucepan for the whole family. I love the way the eggs bake in these cupcake cases – such a novel way to poach an egg. If you don't fancy eggs or your little one is allergic, you could use some tofu instead – crumble it up, drizzle with oil and rub to coat. Bake for 10 minutes and serve with the tomato sauce.

1 tbsp olive oil, plus extra for greasing
4 large free-range eggs (1 egg per
    person)
1 tsp dried oregano
30g greens (such as baby leaf spinach
    or kale)
1 small white onion, peeled and finely
    chopped
400g tin chopped tomatoes
toasted bread or wholemeal pitta,
    to serve

1. Preheat the oven to 200°C/180°C fan.

2. Using a little oil, grease 4 holes in a cupcake tray (or fewer depending on how many people you're serving) then crack in the eggs, sprinkle with a little of the oregano and bake for 10 minutes.

3. Meanwhile, prepare the greens: if using kale, wash, remove the woody stalks and finely chop the leaves; if using spinach, wash and roughly chop.

4. Heat the oil in a medium saucepan over a medium heat, add the onion and cook for 5 minutes, stirring regularly. Add the tomatoes, a good splash of water, the rest of the oregano and the greens. Stir to combine, then bring to the boil, turn down to a simmer and allow the sauce to bubble away and thicken for 5–8 minutes.

5. Once the eggs are cooked, carefully remove them from the tray and serve on top of the tomato sauce with some toasted wholemeal pitta bread soldiers or just simple toast.

Don't worry if your eggs are a little soft inside – that's OK for toddlers, as long as the eggs are Red Lion stamped.

RASPBERRY CHIA SEED JAM

Prep: 2 minutes
Cook: 10 minutes
Makes: about 180ml

Chia seeds have recently become a bit of a staple in my house as I've been using them a lot when experimenting with dairy-free recipes. You don't need a lot, but these little seeds do pack a seriously good nutritional profile with plenty of fibre, omega-3s, healthy fats and minerals. You don't need to grind them and they make a great addition to lots of recipes – they work amazingly as a thickener and egg replacement. I always have some chia seeds in my cupboard these days. This recipe makes a delicious, sweet jam with lots of other flavour notes too. It can be used on toast, dolloped into porridge or even stirred through cream cheese and used as a dip for breadsticks or crackers.

150g fresh raspberries
3 tsp chia seeds
50ml apple juice not from concentrate (optional – if you don't have apple juice you can use another 50ml water, the jam will just be less sweet)
50ml water

1. Wash the raspberries and mash them in a saucepan. Add the chia seeds, apple juice (if using) and water, giving it a stir.

2. On a medium heat, gradually bring to the boil for about 5 minutes, then mash the mixture with a potato masher. Stir to form a lovely jammy sauce and cook for a further 5 minutes.

3. Leave to cool and transfer to a sterilised jar. Store in the fridge for 3–5 days until needed.

AVOCADO ON TOAST

V A

Prep: 5 minutes
Cook: 8 minutes
Serves: 2 toddlers

Avocado on toast has always been a regular meal in our house, though Raffy has recently decided he doesn't like avocado (what?!). Ada loves it, though, so I've started experimenting with it more in recipes. Avo on toast is popular with lots of kids and is great as a savoury brekkie option. The milled seeds add nutrients and texture, and the roasted tomatoes and feta add a zing of flavour to mix in with the creamy avocado. Make sure the feta is pasteurised and use just a small amount as it's pretty salty – a little goes a long way. You can also mix this recipe up a bit and drizzle on some raspberry chia seed jam if you fancy it!

1 ripe avocado, stoned and peeled
squeeze of lemon juice
8 cherry tomatoes on the vine, quartered
drizzle of olive oil
2 slices of wholemeal bread
1 tsp milled seeds
15g feta cheese, crumbled, or dairy-free alternative (optional)

1. Preheat the grill to the highest temperature.

2. Loosely mash the avocado in a bowl. Add a little lemon juice, mix and mash to a nice chunky consistency.

3. Add the tomatoes to a small tray, drizzle with the oil and cook for 8 minutes until slightly softened.

4. Toast the bread and spread with the mashed avocado. Divide the roasted tomatoes between the 2 slices of bread, sprinkle with the milled seeds and finish with a little feta (if using).

A drizzle of olive oil is a good way to add some extra calories and fats for toddlers.

SPINACH MONSTER PANCAKES

Prep: 15 minutes
Cook: 8 minutes
Serves: 2 toddlers

Raffy named this 'Monster Pancake' as it's seriously bright green with red dots all over. This is a fab recipe for getting some veggies in in the morning. This looks amazing with the green spinachy batter – it should hopefully get a bit of a 'wow' from your kids! This is another one that's great as a snack, lunch or even as a party piece. Feel free to use whatever fillings you fancy if you don't have everything I've suggested here: tomatoes and peppers can easily be switched for mushrooms and courgettes, for example.

For the batter
1 large free-range egg or 1 flaxseed egg (see page 109)
100g self-raising flour
80ml milk of choice
handful of spinach (about 80g), washed
olive oil, for cooking

For the topping
6 cherry tomatoes, finely chopped
50g red or yellow pepper, deseeded and finely chopped
30g cheddar cheese, coarsely grated or dairy-free alternative (optional)

1. Preheat the grill to the highest temperature.

2. Add all the batter ingredients to a blender/high-speed mixer and blend to make a thick green batter. Leave to one side.

3. Heat a little olive oil in a 20cm ovenproof non-stick frying pan over a medium heat.

4. Once the pan is hot, pour in all the batter then sprinkle over the topping ingredients. Cook for about 2 minutes, then pop the pan under the grill for 5–6 minutes until the pancake is puffed up and cooked through.

5. Leave to cool a little, then slice into wedges, fingers or squares – whatever you fancy.

Keep any leftover pancakes in the fridge for 2 days or add them to your freezer stash. Simply defrost overnight in the fridge and serve cold, or reheat until hot all the way through.

VEGGIE BREKKIE WRAP

Prep: 10–15 minutes
Cook: 10–15 minutes
Serves: 1 toddler and 2 adults

This is a totally different breakfast option and one that is great for vegetarians and vegans too! Tofu is a good source of nutrients such as protein and iron, and a perfect replacement for meat. It is also versatile and, visually, looks similar to scrambled eggs. If your toddler really isn't into tofu, you can just use 2 free-range eggs instead. I love that this brekkie option is jam-packed with veggies: sweet potato, mushrooms and tomatoes… A great way to start the day!

1 tbsp olive oil
80g chestnut mushrooms, finely sliced
1 large sweet potato (about 200g), peeled and sliced into ½cm rounds (if the sweet potato is really big, cut in half before slicing)
8 cherry tomatoes, quartered
100g firm tofu (calcium-set), drained
large pinch of turmeric
2 wholemeal tortilla wraps
squeeze of lime juice
½ ripe avocado, stoned, peeled, and mashed (optional)

1. Heat the oil in a large frying pan over a medium heat. Add the mushrooms and sweet potato. Cook for 5–10 minutes, stirring now and then, until the mushrooms cook down (liquid released and evaporated) and the potato starts to soften.

2. Add the tomatoes, crumble in the tofu (or crack in the eggs, if using) and add the turmeric. Gently break up the tofu (or eggs) with a spoon and stir while cooking for another 5 minutes.

3. Preheat the oven to 200°C/180°C fan.

4. Keep stirring the tofu mixture so the flavours coat the mushrooms and potato. Check to make sure the sweet potato is super soft. If it is still a little hard, cook for a further few minutes.

5. Put the tortillas in the oven to warm through, then serve filled with the veggie scramble. Squeeze over some lime juice and dollop with a little smashed avocado (if using) before rolling it up to enjoy. You can keep the veggie scramble in the fridge for up to 2 days.

Avocado is such a great addition to meals and can help to add lots of nutrients (B vitamins, fibre) and some healthy fats too. Try mashing or blending it and offering it as a dip, or just offer some slices on the side of your toddler's meal!

Lunch

Lunch in my house has always been a bit 'bish, bash, bosh' with meals put together from fridge raids, and I have to confess it's the one meal I often struggle with inspiration for! That's why I tried to really think outside the box with these options to offer quick, convenient and healthy lunchtime meals that cover a variety of needs: out and about, quick five-minute options, hearty warm meals and even some family favourites too.

Some of these recipes may need the addition of a dip, a side salad or some proteins to make them more balanced, but they are all delicious and I loved creating these to boost your lunchtime inspo. I really hope you enjoy them. Don't forget you can use the ideas in the Snacks section (see pages 182–199) for lunches too – just bulk them out with extra veg, dips or some potatoes, for example!

RAINBOW SALAD AND DRESSING

Prep: 5 minutes
Makes: 1 jar
Serves: 4 toddler portions or
1–2 adult portions

For the dressing
4 tbsp extra-virgin olive oil
juice of ½ lemon
4 tsp English mustard
handful of chives, trimmed and finely
chopped (optional)

For the salad
150g broccoli, coarsely grated
2 medium carrots (about 130g), peeled
and coarsely grated
1 large apple (about 100g), cored and
coarsely grated

This colourful salad is such an easy one to do and can be a great side accompaniment to many meals. The dressing can be kept in the fridge for up to 1 week. It's a really easy way to jazz up a salad without loads of sugar, salt or even effort!

1. To make the dressing, add the oil to a bowl and mix in the lemon juice and mustard. Add the chives (if using) and give it all a good stir. Transfer to a large clean jar and store in the fridge until needed.

2. To make the salad, mix together the broccoli, carrots and apple in a bowl. Squeeze it all together to release the juice of the apple, drizzle with 2–3 tablespoons of the dressing, mix it about a bit and serve.

QUICK RICOTTA TOMATO PASTA

Prep: 5 minutes
Cook: 10 minutes
Serves: 2 toddlers and 1–2 adults

250g wholemeal fusilli (or other pasta
shape)
1 tbsp olive oil
1 garlic clove, peeled and roughly
chopped
3 sprigs of fresh thyme, leaves picked
400g tin chopped tomatoes
large handful of spinach (about 40g),
finely chopped
250g ricotta

Creamy tomato pasta is always a winner in our house, and who doesn't love a pasta dish? Also, ricotta cheese is a lower-salt option, compared to cheddar and feta. This recipe is quick and simple and makes a generous amount.

1. Cook the pasta according to the packet instructions and drain, reserving a little of the starchy pasta water.

2. Heat the oil in a frying pan over a medium heat, then add the garlic and thyme. Cook for 1 minute, then add the tomatoes. Stir through the spinach until it has wilted, then add the ricotta, breaking it up into the sauce.

3. Pour in the hot pasta, adding a little starchy water to bring it all together, stir and serve.

CHEESE AND TOMATO LOAF

Prep: 5 minutes
Cook: 25–30 minutes
Makes: 1 loaf

This is like a mini focaccia (but takes no time at all!) and packs in the flavours. This was a hit when I was doing the recipe testing and is definitely one for the adults as well as the kids; I've even brought it out at a family dinner party recently. As ever with my recipes, you can change up the fillings if you wish. This is delicious (and more balanced) served with some hummus as a dip and some extra veggies or a salad.

250g self-raising flour
1 large free-range egg or 1 chia seed egg (see page 109)
200ml milk of choice
5 spring onions, trimmed and finely sliced
20 cherry tomatoes, quartered
100g cheddar cheese, coarsely grated
drizzle of olive oil

1. Preheat the oven to 200°C/180°C fan. Line a 20cm square ovenproof tin with greaseproof paper.

2. Sift the flour into a bowl and make a well in the middle. In a separate bowl, whisk together the egg and milk. Pour the milk and egg into the well.

3. Whisk the mixture together to combine, then add the spring onions, tomatoes and most of the cheese. Stir to mix in the flavours.

4. Add the mixture to the lined tin, drizzle with a little oil and sprinkle over the reserved cheese. Bake for 25–30 minutes, or until the loaf is brown on top.

5. Leave to cool in the tin for 5 minutes, then carefully lift the loaf from the tin onto a cooling rack. Leave to cool a little before cutting into chunks and serving. This loaf will keep fresh for around 3 days and it is a great addition to your freezer stash. You can grab a few slices and defrost for a couple of hours in time for lunch!

Adding a variety of veggies into home-baked breads and rolls is a good way to get your toddler to try new flavours! Try peppers, courgette or broccoli too.

HOMEMADE BAKED BEANS WITH MINI JACKETS

Prep: 10 minutes
Cook: 30 minutes
Serves: 2 toddlers and 2 adults

My kids and I love filled jacket potatoes – so much! And I'm always asked for an alternative baked beans recipe, and so here is my veg-packed answer to baked beans – you're welcome! The mini jackets in this recipe take less time to cook and are perfectly portioned for little ones – plus they are super cute and kids love them. This recipe is also nice and easy and is a great way to introduce other types of beans and lots of variety for your toddler. You can add some grated cheese and a mini salad to serve, if you wish.

- -

500g baby potatoes, washed
1 tbsp olive oil, plus extra for drizzling
1 garlic clove, peeled and finely chopped
4 spring onions, trimmed and finely chopped
1 celery stick, trimmed and finely grated
1 medium carrot, peeled and finely grated
1 tsp smoked sweet paprika
500g tomato passata
2 x 400g tinned beans, such as cannellini, haricot or butter beans

1. Preheat the oven to 200°C/180°C fan.

2. Add the potatoes to a baking tray, drizzle with oil and roast for 30 minutes until golden, crispy and soft throughout.

3. Meanwhile, to make the beans, heat the oil in a large saucepan over a medium heat. Add the garlic, spring onions, celery and carrot. Cook for 7 minutes, stirring occasionally until softened. Stir in the paprika and cook for 1 minute, then pour in the passata and beans. Cook for a further 8 minutes, stirring now and then.

4. Serve a few tablespoons of beans with the roasted mini jackets. You can always give larger beans a little squash with a fork for toddlers, if needed. Any leftover beans can be kept in the fridge for 2 days or frozen. You can reheat them in the microwave or on the hob, adding a splash of water and stirring regularly, until they are hot all the way through.

Using two types of beans in this recipe adds different textures, more variety and some extra nutrients too.

CHEESY TUNA AND PEA OPEN TOASTIE

Prep: 5 minutes
Cook: 5 minutes
Serves: 2 toddlers and 1 adult

This is a play on cheese on toast but with a fab flavour combo and more variety – just how I like it! These are great served whole for lunch or cut into little fingers as a snack. This recipe is also super quick, so when you need a speedy, varied lunch, you're sorted. Ada loves this recipe and I've also tried it with different types of tinned fish too – sardines are actually Ada's favourite.

50g frozen peas
120g (about) tin tuna or sardines (MSC approved), drained
3 tbsp Greek yoghurt
40g cheddar cheese, grated
pinch of garlic granules
2–3 slices of thick wholemeal bread

1. Cook the peas according to the packet instructions. When cooked, drain and run under cold running water. Transfer the peas to a bowl and mash until chunky.

2. Preheat the grill to the highest temperature.

3. Add the tuna or sardines to the mashed peas, breaking it up with a fork. Mix in the yoghurt, half the cheese and the garlic granules.

4. Lightly toast the bread, then load each slice with the fish mixture. You can spread it as thickly or as thinly as you like.

5. Sprinkle the remaining cheese over the top of the bread slices, place them on a baking tray and grill for 3–4 minutes until the topping is bubbly and golden.

6. Leave to cool a little and cut into triangles or fingers to serve. If you use two slices of bread, you will likely have some tuna mixture leftover – you can store this in the fridge for up to 2 days.

If you want to make this cheese-free, leave out the cheese and simply sprinkle some nutritional yeast on top to give it a cheesy finish!

SWEET POTATO AND BEAN CAKES

Prep: 15 minutes
Cook: 20–30 minutes
Makes: 10 cakes

These are a great alternative to burgers or fishcakes, and are packed with amazing flavours and textures. The bean mashing does take a little work, but it's well worth it, and you can make a batch and keep the mixture in the fridge for the next couple of days or freeze some of the cakes for later. Serve in a bun or just on its own, whichever you fancy!

2 medium sweet potatoes (about 400g)
400g tin kidney beans, drained and rinsed
400g tin cannellini beans, drained and rinsed
1–2 tbsp tomato purée
2 spring onions, trimmed and finely chopped
80g shop-bought or homemade breadcrumbs (see page 109)
2 tbsp olive oil
1 ripe avocado, destoned and skin removed
1 lime

1. Preheat the oven to 200°C/180°C fan. Line a baking tray with greaseproof paper.

2. Wash and scrub the potatoes and prick them on all sides with a fork. Pop them into a microwave for 5 minutes or bake for 1 hour at 200°C/180°C fan until the flesh is soft. Leave to one side.

3. In a bowl mash the beans until they form a paste. Mix in the tomato purée and spring onions and stir until combined. Scoop out the flesh of the cooked potatoes, add to the bowl and mix.

4. Shape the mixture into 10 balls, then flatten into 8cm wide patties.

5. Pour the breadcrumbs onto a plate and dip the patties into the breadcrumbs to coat. Transfer the patties to the tray.

6. Brush each with a little olive oil and bake for 10–15 minutes each side or until golden and hot all the way through.

7. Once the bean cakes are cooked, leave them to cool a little (this also allows them to firm up). Mash the avocado with a good squeeze of lime and serve the beancakes with a dollop of the avocado alongside for dunking for little ones. For older ones and adults, spread some on top of the cake.

You can crumble in a little cheese when you mash the beans, which helps to add some extra flavour, but it's not necessary.

MINI BROCCOLI TORTILLA WRAP QUICHES

Prep: 8 minutes
Cook: 8–10 minutes
Makes: 12 mini quiches

Ada loves a quiche, but they can be super fiddly to make and if you buy them when you're out and about they often contain lots of added salt. I therefore wanted to come up with a great quiche option that is quick and convenient, and these have been such a hit! These are great for lunches, parties or even munching when out and about. The filling can be easily changed up with things you have leftover in the fridge, so feel free to swap in some other veggies – enjoy!

unsalted butter, dairy-free spread or oil, for greasing
2–3 large wholemeal tortilla wraps
80g broccoli, trimmed and roughly chopped, stalks finely chopped
6 cherry tomatoes, quartered
3 large free-range eggs
1 tbsp nutritional yeast

1. Preheat the oven to 200°C/180°C fan. Grease a 12-hole muffin tray.

2. Using a large cup (or cutter if you have one), cut out 12 x 9cm circles from the wraps (you should get about 4 per wrap).

3. Pop the wrap circles into each hole of the muffin tray to create a little cup.

4. Put the broccoli, tomatoes, eggs and nutritional yeast into a high-speed blender. Blitz for a second to cut it all up to a good texture (you can keep it chunkier for older kids if you prefer).

5. Carefully divide the veggie mixture into each cupcake hole (being careful that it doesn't spill over the edges) and bake for 8–10 minutes or until cooked and golden. Leave to cool and set a little on a cooling rack before serving. Any leftover quiches can be frozen or kept in the fridge for 2 days and can be served hot or cold.

Nutritional yeast adds a cheesy flavour and also some additional nutrients, such as B vitamins. You don't need much – a little goes a long way flavour-wise!

NUGGETS WITH HERBY CHIPS

A ❄

Prep: 15 minutes
Cook: 1 hour
Serves: 2 toddlers and 2 adults

Who doesn't like a healthier take on chicken (or tofu!) nuggets and chips? This recipe takes a little longer to cook, but it is such a fun one for toddlers to get involved with too. It's easy to make this dish vegan by using tofu and dipping in flax/chia seed instead of egg. I made this with Raffy and he loved the tofu nuggets!

- -

3 large baking potatoes (about 800g), washed

150g shop-bought or homemade (see page 109) breadcrumbs

1 tsp smoked sweet paprika

2 large free-range eggs, beaten, or 2 chia seed eggs (see page 109)

3 tbsp olive oil

½ tbsp mixed dried herbs

2 large free-range skinless and boneless chicken breasts (about 450g) or 2 sustainable white fish fillets, boned and skinned (coley, hake or haddock work well) or 280g firm tofu, cut into 3cm chunks

cooked broccoli, to serve

> Adding herbs and spices to meals is a fab way to jazz up dishes and add some extra flavours as well as a little sprinkle of nutrition. I love using paprika, cumin, oregano and basil in our family meals!

1. Bring a large pan of water to the boil. Cut the potatoes into 2cm thick finger-shaped chips. Put the potatoes into the pan and boil for 6–8 minutes. Drain and leave to steam dry in the colander for 2 minutes.

2. Meanwhile, get two shallow bowls. Place the breadcrumbs into one and mix in the paprika. Put the beaten eggs into the other.

3. Preheat the oven to 200°C/180°C fan. Line a roasting tin with greaseproof paper.

4. Pour the oil into the roasting tin, add the chips, sprinkle over the mixed herbs and toss to coat. Cook in the oven for 30–40 minutes until golden and crisp, turning halfway through.

5. Dip the chicken, fish or tofu into the egg mixture, shaking off any excess. Then dip into the breadcrumbs, patting and squashing the chicken, fish or tofu to flatten it a little and to make sure all sides are covered.

6. Add the chicken, fish or tofu to a baking tray in one layer and bake for 10–15 minutes until cooked through.

7. Serve the nuggets and chips with some cooked broccoli.

LENTIL AND BEEF BALLS

Prep: 20 minutes
Cook: 20 minutes
Serves: 2 toddlers and 2 adults
plus an extra batch of balls

This is a twist on the classic meatball dish, but with lentils and veggies in the mix to add extra fibre and textures. It packs in flavour and adds variety, and you can freeze the meatballs and the sauce, so that lunch or dinner is as simple as boiling some pasta!

For the beef balls

1 red onion, peeled and roughly chopped
2 garlic cloves, peeled
5 sprigs of fresh rosemary, leaves picked
500g good-quality beef
50g shop-bought or homemade breadcrumbs (see page 109)
500g cooked Puy lentils
good pinch of ground cumin
good pinch of sweet paprika
30g Parmesan cheese, grated, plus extra for serving
drizzle of olive oil

For the tomato sauce

1 tbsp olive oil
1 courgette, trimmed and grated
1 medium carrot, peeled and coarsely grated
½ bunch of fresh basil (15g), stalks and most of the leaves finely chopped, baby leaves picked and reserved
400g tin chopped tomatoes
freshly ground black pepper

1. In a food processor, add the onion, garlic and rosemary and blend until finely chopped. Add the mince and pulse a few times to roughly blend.

2. Add the breadcrumbs and lentils, along with the spices and Parmesan and pulse until just combined (you want to keep some of the lentils whole).

3. Wet your hands, then roughly divide the meat mixture in half. Divide one half into 24 balls and freeze the other half for another day.

4. Heat a drizzle of oil in a large frying pan over a medium heat. Add the meatballs and fry until evenly cooked all the way through and no pink meat remains. Transfer to a bowl and set to one side.

5. To make the sauce, put the frying pan back on the heat and add the oil along with the courgette, carrot, basil stalks and most of the chopped leaves. Cook for 3–4 minutes until softened.

6. Pour the tomatoes into the frying pan, adding one third of a tin of hot water. Stir and cook for 5 minutes. Add the beef balls to the sauce and cook for another 5 minutes. You can serve these with cooked pasta and a little grating of cheese on top.

SPEEDY PORK RICE STIR-FRY

𝒜

Prep: 5 minutes
Cook: 10–15 minutes
Serves: 2 toddlers and 1 adult

Stir-fries can make such an easy, speedy and balanced lunch for families, and I often find myself wondering why I don't make them more often. This one is especially easy as it uses frozen veggies, but you can always just throw in any leftovers you have in the fridge instead! For younger toddlers you could give all these ingredients a little mash at the end, if needed, but most of them should be nice and soft for your little ones.

1 tbsp vegetable oil
2 garlic cloves, peeled and finely chopped
4 spring onions, trimmed and finely sliced
250g pork mince (or 400g tin black beans, drained)
1 tsp Chinese five-spice powder
250g frozen mixed colourful veg (such as peppers, sweetcorn and frozen peas)
1 large free-range egg, beaten (optional)
250g bag of pre-cooked rice
1 tbsp low-salt soy sauce (optional)

1. Place a large wok (or frying pan) on a high heat.

2. Add the oil, garlic, spring onions, pork mince (if using) and five-spice powder. Cook for a minute or so, then add the frozen veg and cook for another 5 minutes, moving it all about to get the veg soft and the pork crispy.

3. Add the rice pouch, black beans (if using instead of the pork) and egg (if using) and cook for another 5 minutes, until piping hot and cooked through.

4. Stir in the soy sauce (if using) and serve. Cool any leftovers quickly, within 1 hour, and store in the fridge. Use within 24 hours.

Swap out the veggies for whatever you have available – stir-fries are a great way to use up leftover fresh veg and can help you become more confident with experimenting too!

Dinner

Dinners are often so much more complex with families, aren't they? Eating together, eating separately, cooking in the evening when everyone is tired and hungry. So often they can be chaotic – they sure are in my house! It's fine for dinners to sometimes be cold buffets of what you have left over in the fridge or thrown-together meals that don't usually 'go'. I often rely on savoury porridge, omelettes or cereal if we've had a busy day and I can't think of anything else to make.

However, most of the dinner recipes in this section are fairly easy family meals that everyone can enjoy. Most are pretty quick to put together, which is why I've focused on a few traybakes, just to make life a little easier in the evening. These can also be great options to make at the weekend or in bulk and freeze, so all you have to do is reheat and dinner is served! Sound like bliss? Read on!

QUICK RATATOUILLE-STYLE ORZO

V A ❄

Prep: 15 minutes
Cook: 25–30 minutes
Serves: 2 toddlers and 2 adults
with leftovers for another day

Orzo is a great staple to have in your dry store cupboard. It cooks quickly and is a lovely alternative to rice or the larger pasta shapes. Ratatouille is a classic for my family, but I wanted to use it in a different way in this recipe. I thought orzo combined with ratatouille would work well and it really does! There are plenty of veggies in this one and it's an easy, fun dish to make for the whole family.

1 tbsp olive oil
1 garlic clove, peeled and finely chopped
1 aubergine, finely chopped
½ red or yellow pepper, deseeded and finely chopped
2 heaped tsp dried oregano
small bunch of basil, leaves picked and finely chopped, stalks finely chopped
1 courgette, trimmed and grated
400g tin chopped tomatoes
200g orzo
200ml water or 200ml vegetable stock (low- or zero salt)
2 handfuls of pine nuts (or other nuts), ground to a fine powder if for little ones, kept whole for adults
25g finely grated cheddar cheese or dairy-free alternative (optional)

1. Heat the oil in a large pan over a medium heat. Add the garlic, aubergine, pepper, oregano and basil stalks. Cook for 5 minutes, stirring occasionally, then add the courgette and cook for a further 5 minutes until softened and browning.

2. Next, add the tomatoes, orzo, stock (or water), plus a 400ml tin of water, and continue cooking for 12–15 minutes until the liquid is mostly absorbed and it has thickened to a nice sauce consistency. Add an extra splash or two of water if the sauce is drying up too quickly before it is cooked through.

3. Take off the heat, stir in the basil leaves and serve with the remaining nuts and/or some grated cheese. Leftovers can be stored in the fridge for 2 days or can be frozen for up to 3 months. Thoroughly defrost before reheating in the pan with a splash of water until hot all the way through.

Ground nuts make a great topping for recipes and also help to add extra nutrients such as iron and zinc, without really altering the flavour too much.

LEMON AND LENTIL CREAMY PASTA

V A ❄

Prep: 10 minutes
Cook: 20 minutes
Serves: 2 toddlers and 2 adults
          with leftovers for another day

This recipe was really for me! I love creamy sauces – my dad made me a lemon-flavoured one and I just had to recreate it! This flavour combo – lentils with a creamy lemon sauce – just seems to work so well. I hope your little ones like this too. I often use the pre-cooked pouches of lentils as they are so quick and simple; Puy lentils are my favourite as they are really versatile.

1 tbsp olive oil
3 leeks (about 400g), cleaned and
    finely sliced
3 sprigs of fresh thyme, leaves picked,
    or ½ tsp dried thyme
240g pasta shapes (fettuccine or
    rigatoni work well)
1 tbsp unsalted butter or dairy-free
    spread
1 heaped tbsp plain flour
400ml milk of choice
grated zest of 1 lemon and juice of ½
½ x 250g pouch Puy lentils
15g Parmesan or dairy-free alternative
    (optional)

1. Heat the oil in a large saucepan over a medium heat. Add the leeks and thyme and cook for 10–12 minutes until the leeks are sweet and sticky, stirring occasionally.

2. Meanwhile, cook the pasta according to the packet instructions and drain, reserving a little of the starchy pasta water.

3. Add the butter or spread to the pan with the leeks, allow it to melt, then add the flour and stir to combine. Slowly add the milk, stirring continuously until thickened. Then add the lemon zest and juice. Tip in the lentils, give it all a stir to combine and warm through.

4. Pour the hot pasta into the creamy lentil sauce and mix in most of the Parmesan (if using). If the sauce seems too thick, add a splash of the reserved pasta water to loosen it. You can keep any leftovers in the fridge for 2 days or store them in the freezer.

Lentils are such a great food and I love chucking half a packet into meals that I make at home. This is a great way of adding some extra nutrients such as B vitamins, zinc and iron for the whole family.

BEETROOT RISOTTO

V A

Prep: 15 minutes
Cook: 30–35 minutes
Serves: 2 toddlers and 2 adults
with leftovers for another day

I really love a colourful recipe and this one is no exception – purple risotto! Hopefully this is one that will get the kids excited too! Cooking risotto always takes a little more time as you have to stand stirring the rice, so I think it's often best to do this one without the kids circling your feet. It has a nice, subtle flavour and is a great way to offer beetroot in a different way.

1 bulb of fennel (about 200g), roughly chopped
1 white onion, peeled
2 celery sticks
2 garlic cloves, peeled
1 tbsp olive oil
6 sprigs of fresh thyme, leaves picked
250g risotto rice
3 balls vacuum-packed beetroot (about 120g) in natural juices, drained (reserve the liquid) and blended
1 litre boiling water
50g mature cheddar cheese or dairy-free alternative, grated
½ x 400g tin butter beans, drained and roughly chopped (optional)

1. Add the fennel, onion, celery and garlic to a food processor and pulse until finely chopped. Heat 1 tablespoon of the oil in a large non-stick pan over a medium heat and add the pulsed veg mixture to the pan, along with the thyme leaves. Cook for 5 minutes until softened, stirring now and then.

2. Add the rice and cook for another 2 minutes, then add 80ml of the beetroot juices (or a splash of water if you don't have any liquid left).

3. Allow the liquid to evaporate, then add a ladleful of the boiling water, making sure you keep stirring until the liquid has all been absorbed. Keep adding ladlefuls, stirring all the time, until all the liquid has been absorbed and the rice is soft – this will take 25–30 minutes – adding the blended beetroot for the last 10 minutes.

4. Add the cheese and butter beans (if using) and stir, then pop a lid on for a final 5 minutes. Cool any leftovers as quickly as possible, within 1 hour of cooking, and store in the fridge. Use within 24 hours.

Adding flavours and textures is so easy. You can usually add ground nuts, a squeeze of lemon or lime, a sprinkling of cheese or some toasted breadcrumbs to add extras to your dinners!

CHICKEN KATSU CURRY

A ❄

Prep: 15 minutes
Cook: 20 minutes
Serves: 2 adults and 2 toddlers

My family and I love a curry! If you don't eat chicken, here you can easily replace it with tofu. This recipe takes a little more concentration, but you can prep the sauce and get ahead with the coating so you can just bake the chicken/tofu when you're ready to eat it. There are plenty of flavours and textures in this recipe – I hope it ends up as a family staple for you like it has in our house!

· ·

1 tbsp olive oil
1 white onion, peeled and roughly chopped
2 garlic cloves, peeled and chopped
1 medium carrot, peeled and coarsely grated
½ tsp ground ginger
2 tsp mild curry powder (no added salt)
1 heaped tbsp plain flour, plus 80g for coating
200ml tinned coconut milk
2 free-range skinless and boneless chicken breasts (about 420g), cut into 3cm thick strips, or 280g calcium-set tofu, cut into squares
2 large free-range eggs, beaten, or 2 chia seed eggs (see page 109)
150g shop-bought or homemade breadcrumbs (see page 109)
cooked white rice, to serve
cooked frozen veg medley (pea, broccoli and sweetcorn mix), to serve

1. To make the sauce, heat the oil in a pan over a medium heat. Add the onion, garlic and carrot and cook for 8–10 minutes until softened (but not coloured), stirring occasionally.

2. Add the ginger and curry powder and stir to combine, then add the flour and mix to form a paste. Remove the pan from the heat and place the mixture into a blender with 100ml of the coconut milk. Blend to a thick, smooth sauce.

3. Return the mixture to the pan, add the remaining coconut milk, stir and bring to the boil. Preheat the oven to 220°C/200°C fan.

4. Lightly bash the chicken to flatten. Get three shallow bowls. Put the flour into one, the beaten egg into another and the breadcrumbs into the final bowl. Dip the chicken (or tofu) pieces into the flour first, shaking off the excess, then into the egg. Hold it up to let the excess egg drip off, then dip it into the breadcrumbs.

5. Put the coated chicken or tofu on a large baking tray and bake for 8–10 minutes, turning halfway through, or until golden and cooked through.

6. Serve with white rice and medley veg.

TURKISH-STYLE BEEF SKEWERS

Prep: 10 minutes
Cook: 15 minutes
Makes: 12 skewers

I like helping toddlers to experiment with different foods from around the globe and so these beef skewers (or koftas) made a simple and slightly experimental recipe for me. If you don't have skewers, don't worry – just mould the beef into rough balls and fry as normal. Remove the meat from the skewers for little ones before serving.

· ·

1 small red onion, peeled and roughly chopped
½ a bunch of fresh mint, leaves picked and finely chopped
400g good-quality beef mince
1 red or yellow pepper, halved, deseeded and roughly chopped
plain flour, for dusting
1 tsp ground cumin
1 tsp sweet smoked paprika
200g wholewheat couscous
juice and grated zest of 1 lemon
1 tbsp olive oil
1 cucumber, cut into lengthway fingers, to serve
yoghurt, to serve
large handful of ground pistachios (optional), to serve

1. Put the red onion and half the mint leaves into a food processor. Blitz until chopped up finely, then add the beef mince and pepper and blend again to combine. Place the mixture into a bowl, add the spices and stir.

2. With flour-dusted hands, shape the mixture into 12 golf ball-sized balls. Push a wooden skewer through each ball and squash the ball into a rough sausage shape (about 8cm long).

3. Put the skewers in the fridge for 30 minutes to firm up while you make the couscous.

4. Cook the couscous according to the packet instructions. Once cooked, stir in the lemon zest, juice and remaining mint, then set to one side.

5. To cook the skewers, heat the oil in a large frying pan over a medium heat. Carefully place the skewers in the pan and fry for 7–8 minutes, turning them around until they are cooked evenly and no pink meat remains.

6. Serve with the couscous, cucumber, a dollop of yoghurt and a sprinkle of pistachios (if using).

Surplus skewers can be frozen raw (just stop at step 3), or once cooked. To reheat, defrost them thoroughly and place on a pan over medium heat until they are cooked all the way through.

SALMON BURGERS WITH KALE SALSA

Prep: 20 minutes
Cook: 10–15 minutes
Makes: 4 large or 6 mini burgers

My two love this recipe! It was the first burger that Ada had ever tried and she was pretty good at holding it too. I love a nutritious and novelty burger recipe and this one really is so different and simple! It's pretty quick to prep and can easily be deconstructed and eaten as separate parts for younger toddlers who can't quite manage the burger shape. The kale salsa is an added bonus, adding some variety, flavour and crispy, crunchy deliciousness.

- -

30g kale, stalks removed, leaves trimmed and torn into small pieces
1 tbsp olive oil, plus extra for drizzling
4 wholemeal burger buns (or 6 mini ones for the kids)
6 cherry tomatoes, finely chopped
½ apple, cored and finely sliced into matchsticks
juice of 1 lemon
1 tbsp dried oregano
4 tbsp plain flour
3 x 120g sustainable skinless and boneless salmon fillets, cut into 2cm thick sticks
1 ripe avocado, stoned peeled and mashed (or use the Green Dip on page 195)

1. Preheat the oven to 200°C/180°C fan.

2. Place the kale onto a baking tray and drizzle with 1 tablespoon of the oil. Cook in the oven for 5 minutes until crispy. Toast the burger buns in the oven until golden. Mix the crispy kale with the tomatoes and apple, and dress with a little lemon juice.

3. Mix the oregano with the flour in a medium bowl. Toss the salmon in the oregano flour.

4. Heat a drizzle of olive oil in a large non-stick frying pan over medium heat. Place the salmon pieces in the pan and cook for 5–8 minutes, flipping occasionally until golden and cooked through on both sides.

5. To assemble the burgers, spread a little of the mashed avocado on a bun base, then add the fish pieces and some crispy kale and tomato salsa. These burgers are delicious served with the homemade Herby Chips on page 140. You can store any leftover cooked fish in the fridge for 2 days or in the freezer for up to 2 months.

Salsas are a great way to add extra colour, nutrients, fibre and excitement to dishes for kids. Raffy loved picking at the salsa in this one and came back for a few more portions!

CREAMY CHICKPEA CAULIFLOWER CHEESE

V A ❄

Prep: 5–10 minutes
Cook: 30 minutes
Serves: 2 toddlers and 2 adults
            with leftovers for another day

Another winner for my family, this recipe is a bit like macaroni cheese – a favourite in our house – but with some added extras. Chickpeas are a great source of protein and iron, and cauliflower is a lovely flavour mixed with the cumin. Ada is such a fan of creamy sauces, so I tend to use them fairly frequently! You can mash the mixture down a bit more for younger toddlers or keep it chunkier for adults and older kids.

• •

1 medium cauliflower (about 500g), trimmed and cut into chunks
300g colourful pasta shapes
1 tbsp unsalted butter or dairy-free spread
1 small courgette, roughly chopped
2 tbsp plain flour
1 tsp ground cumin
600ml milk of choice
400g tin butter beans, drained
400g tin chickpeas, drained
120g mature cheddar cheese or dairy-free alternative
2 tbsp milled seeds

1. Bring a large pan of water to the boil. Parboil the cauliflower and pasta for 5 minutes. Drain, reserving a good mugful of the water and put to one side. Keep the pan for making the sauce.

2. To make the creamy sauce, add the butter or spread into the pan, allow it to melt, then add the courgette, cooking for 5 minutes.

3. Add the flour and ground cumin, and stir to combine. Slowly add the milk, stirring continuously until thickened, then pour in the beans and chickpeas, mashing up a little if needed.

4. Mix the cooked pasta and cauliflower into the sauce and stir in 100g of the cheddar, then pour into a roasting tin, top with the rest of the cheddar and sprinkle over the milled seeds.

5. Cover with foil and cook for 10 minutes, then uncover and cook for a further 15 minutes until golden and a little bit crispy. You can freeze any leftovers. To reheat, defrost thoroughly and place in the oven until they are hot all the way through.

Adding dairy to dinners is a great way to get some calcium in for toddlers, especially if they aren't so keen on drinking milk.

BUTTERNUT SQUASH AND BUTTER BEAN TRAY BAKE

Prep: 15 minutes
Cook: 25–35 minutes
Serves: 2 toddlers and 2 adults
          with leftovers for another day

This has a really Moroccan vibe to it and helps to introduce your toddler to some new flavours and light spices, while also being sweet and comforting. This recipe can also work well as a side dish and is great as an accompaniment to meat or fish. Giant couscous is also useful to have in the dry store cupboard and is often quite a fun one to offer to the kids.

. . . .

1kg butternut squash, peeled, deseeded and cut into 2cm pieces
1½ tsp ground cinnamon
1½ tsp garam masala
1 tbsp olive oil
125g giant couscous/pearl barley
200g green beans, trimmed and cut into 1cm pieces
400g tin butter beans, drained and roughly chopped
2 handfuls of dried apricots, very finely chopped

Younger toddlers might need a bit of help with this one. Try offering the green beans as finger foods and giving the rest a bit of a mash before serving.

1. Preheat the oven to 200°C/180°C fan.

2. Place the butternut squash into a large roasting tin, scatter over the spices and drizzle with the olive oil. Rub it all together to mix the flavours. Put into the oven to roast for 15 minutes.

3. Meanwhile, cook the couscous according to the packet instructions, adding the green beans for the final 5 minutes. Drain and set aside.

4. When the squash has been in the oven for about 15 minutes, add to the roasting tin the butter beans, couscous and green beans. Return to the oven for a further 10 minutes (or until the squash is cooked through).

5. Remove from the oven, sprinkle over the dried apricots and a little extra oil, and serve. You can keep any leftovers in the fridge for up to 2 days.

WHITE FISH AND ORANGE TRAYBAKE

Prep: 10 minutes
Cook: 35 minutes
Makes: 2 toddlers and 2 adults

In my first book, my Creamy Lemony Salmon Bake was so popular, so I wanted to create another simple and easy traybake for this book that packed in plenty of flavour and included fish. Voilà – here it is. It's so easy to offer parts of this traybake for your toddler to feed themselves, or mash it all up a little, if needed. This dish is jam-packed with veg and can be switched up during different seasons. The orange and crème fraîche combo also makes a lovely creamy sauce.

450g new potatoes, washed and halved (cut any really big ones into quarters)
1 sweet potato (about 150g), washed and cut into rough chunks
150g cherry tomatoes, halved
1 yellow pepper, deseeded and cut into strips
1 tbsp olive oil, plus extra for drizzling
200g crème fraîche
juice and grated zest of 1 orange
2 x 140g skinless, boneless white fish fillets, cut into 5cm pieces
handful of chopped spinach leaves, to serve (optional)
5g dill, finely chopped (optional)

1. Preheat the oven to 220°C/200°C fan.

2. Place the new potatoes and sweet potato into a roasting tin. Add the tomatoes and peppers, drizzle with oil and roast for 20–25 minutes until the potatoes are soft and golden.

3. Meanwhile, mix the crème fraîche with the orange zest and juice.

4. Dollop the orange crème fraîche all over the veggies, then dot the fish pieces around the tin. Drizzle with a little more oil and pop the tin back in the oven for 8–10 minutes (depending on the thickness of the fish fillets).

5. Once cooked, add a handful of chopped spinach leaves (if using) allowing them to wilt through the mix. Serve with dill (if using). This dish is best eaten fresh, but any leftovers can be safely kept in the fridge for 2 days.

Lemons, limes and oranges make such great flavour additions and are a handy way of replacing the need for salt and sugar. We love flavouring using citrus in our house.

PRAWN, PEPPER AND KIDNEY BEAN NACHO TRAYBAKE

A

Prep: 10 minutes
Cook: 25–30 minutes
Serves: 2 toddlers and 2 adults

I've always loved nachos and this is a great recipe that's ideal for small children too. This is a really easy nacho dinner that all the family will love. It's also super easy to adapt: you can use chicken, add avocado and soured cream; substitute the prawns with tofu and use a vegan cheese alternative; or even use the sauce for pasta or potato toppings.

· ·

2 large wholewheat tortilla wraps, cut into nacho-like wedges
1 tbsp olive oil
1 red or yellow pepper, deseeded and cut into 3cm chunks
1 red onion, peeled and cut into small wedges
2 garlic cloves, peeled and finely chopped
400g tin chopped tomatoes
200g fresh king prawns (or defrosted if frozen) or 280g tofu, drained
400g tin kidney beans, drained
50g cheddar cheese or dairy-free alternative, grated

1. Preheat the oven to 200°C/180°C fan.

2. Spread out the nacho wedges on a shallow baking tray and drizzle with half the oil. Set aside.

3. Place the pepper, onion and garlic into a roasting tin and drizzle with the remaining oil. Cook for 15 minutes.

4. Remove the veg from the oven, add the tomatoes, prawns (or tofu) and kidney beans, and give it all a good stir. Cook for a further 10–15 minutes until the prawns are cooked through and the sauce is thickened.

5. Bake the tray of nacho wedges at the same time for 5 minutes until crispy, then add the cheese on top of the nachos and bake for another couple of minutes until the cheese has melted.

6. Give little ones a portion of the sauce with a few cheesy nachos for dunking. Chop or mash the sauce for younger toddlers if the chunky veggies are too much for them to manage.

Celebrations

Celebrations for children are always filled with sweets, cakes and biscuits, and there isn't anything wrong with enjoying these foods. But what if celebration events weren't *just* about sugary foods and we used them to try to celebrate all the foods and flavours we have available and that our kids love?

I think it's so easy to make lots of foods – savoury, sweet, bitter – as fun for kids as those cakes and sweets. My idea for this section of the book is to offer some lower-sugar alternatives for those families that want these options at birthdays, but also to show how lots of other foods and recipes are perfect for times of celebration too.

Some of these recipes use plenty of dairy, but it's often easy to leave it out (for example, when it's suggested as a serving option) or swap with alternatives such as coconut yoghurt or other non-dairy options.

I've included some amazing sandwich fillers, pizza toppings, snack options and some 'healthier' offerings for puddings and cakes. I hope you like them. My two loved trying these!

BUILD YOUR OWN PIZZAS

V A

Prep: 15 – 20 minutes
Cook: 10 minutes
Makes: 4 standard or 8 mini pizzas

We're big fans of pizza in our house and regularly have this, so I wanted to go one step further here and give a great pizza recipe with some fab topping ideas that will cater for everyone's needs. It's also a super-simple dough recipe that doesn't need proving for hours as it uses self-raising flour and can be whipped up in 15–20 minutes.

For the pizza base

300g self-raising flour, plus extra for dusting
300g natural yoghurt or dairy-free alternative
2 tbsp extra-virgin olive oil
plain flour, for dusting
handful of fine polenta

> Any leftover pizza slices can be kept in the fridge for up to 2 days and reheated until hot all the way through. You can also freeze any extra dough at step 3 before it's cooked and thaw the dough overnight in the fridge before use.

1. Preheat the grill to the highest temperature. Place a large baking sheet on the top shelf of the oven so it gets nice and hot.

2. Have all your chosen toppings in bowls ready to top the pizzas (see opposite).

3. Mix the ingredients for the pizza base in a bowl. When the dough comes together and is less sticky, place it on a well-dusted flour surface and knead for 3–4 minutes until it is lovely and smooth.

4. Divide the dough into four large balls (or eight mini), then shape and roll into rough circles (dusting the rolling pin and dough with more flour as you go to stop it sticking).

5. Sprinkle the preheated tray with a little fine polenta to stop the pizza sticking, then place the rolled dough base onto the tray, being careful as the tray will be hot. Follow the instructions opposite for your chosen pizza.

6. Cook for 5–6 minutes, or until golden and crispy and the toppings look delicious.

7. Cut into slices, serve on a big board and let everyone get stuck in!

The cheesy one

10g cheddar cheese, grated
10g red Leicester cheese, grated
30g pre-grated mozzarella
4 tbsp passata

1. Put the cheeses into a bowl and mix together.

2. Once the base is on the preheated tray, quickly spread the passata onto it, leaving a 1cm border around the edge.

3. Sprinkle over the cheeses and cook as per the instructions opposite.

. . . .

The vegan one

4 tbsp passata
30g vegan cheese, grated (vegan mozzarella works really well)
20g mushrooms, finely sliced
30g red or yellow pepper, sliced
1 heaped tbsp slightly smashed chickpeas (optional)

1. Once the base is on the preheated tray, quickly spread the passata onto it, leaving a 1cm border around the edge.

2. Sprinkle over the cheese and scatter over the mushrooms, pepper and chickpeas (if using). Cook as per the instructions opposite.

. . . .

The green one

4 tbsp pesto (or 4 tbsp passata)
30g pre-grated mozzarella
20g spinach, roughly chopped
30g courgette, trimmed and coarsely grated
1 large free-range egg (optional)

1. Once the base is on the preheated tray, quickly spread the pesto (or passata) onto it, leaving a 1cm border around the edge.

2. Sprinkle over the mozzarella, spinach and courgette, and crack the egg on top (if using). Cook as per the instructions opposite, making sure the egg is cooked.

. . . .

The wild one

2 tbsp passata
½ tsp smoked paprika
35g pre-grated mozzarella
30g cooked chicken, shredded
2 tbsp tinned sweetcorn, drained

1. Mix the passata with the smoked paprika.

2. Once the base is on the preheated tray, quickly spread the passata onto it, leaving a 1cm border around the edge.

3. Sprinkle over the cheese, cooked chicken and sweetcorn, and cook as per the instructions opposite.

SANDWICH FILLERS

V A ❄

Prep: 5–15 minutes
Makes: 8 mini sandwiches

When it comes to sandwiches, they really don't have to be the standard cheese, ham or jam! Here you'll find some different, varied and exciting options that would be perfect for any party occasion! With smooth toppings you can even get creative and use cutters to make fun shapes, which help add a little extra to the party spread (time allowing, of course!).

. . . .

Avocado and hummus

4 slices of wholemeal sliced bread
unsalted butter, at room temperature, or dairy-free spread
½ ripe avocado, stoned, peeled and mashed
2 tbsp hummus

1. Butter one side of each bread slice and place them buttered side up on a board.

2. Spread two bread slices with the mashed avocado and hummus, and top with the remaining bread slices.

3. Cut into triangles, fingers or whatever shape you fancy!

. . . .

Cream cheese, beetroot and fennel

4 slices of wholemeal sliced bread
unsalted butter, at room temperature, or dairy-free spread
1 ball vacuum-packed beetroot (in natural juices), drained and grated
70g fennel, finely grated
2 tbsp cream cheese or dairy-free alternative

1. Butter one side of each bread slice and place them buttered side up on a board.

2. Mix the beetroot and fennel in a bowl and stir in the cream cheese.

3. Spread two bread slices with the beetroot and fennel mixture and top with the remaining bread slices.

4. Cut into triangles, fingers or whatever shape you fancy!

Cottage cheese, baked peaches and cinnamon

240g tin peach slices, drained
juice of ½ orange
pinch of ground cinnamon
4 slices of wholemeal sliced bread
unsalted butter, at room temperature, or dairy-free spread
2 tbsp cottage cheese

1. Preheat the oven to 200°C/180°C fan.

2. Put the peach slices into a roasting tin. Squeeze over the orange juice and sprinkle on the cinnamon. Bake for 15 minutes until the peach slices are soft and sticky. Leave to cool then mash.

3. Butter one side of each bread slice and place them buttered side up on a board. Spread two bread slices with cottage cheese and two slices with 2 tablespoons of mashed peach (you don't want to overfill so save the rest for another time). Sandwich the slices together and cut into triangles, fingers or whatever shape you fancy!

 Any leftover filling for these recipes can be kept in the fridge and used within 2 days.

KIWI SORBET

Prep: 5 minutes,
        plus 5 hours' freezing time
Makes: a small tub

6 very ripe kiwis, skins removed, flesh cut into chunks
1 small ripe banana
2 tbsp coconut yoghurt
juice of ½ orange

This recipe is so refreshing, and it's so simple that your toddler can help you make it! Serve it up in cones or in little dishes for them to get stuck into. Ideally use super-ripe kiwis or the sorbet might end up a little sour. My two love this recipe and it's now a staple that we offer at Grandma and Grandpa's house!

1. Add the kiwis, banana, coconut yoghurt and orange juice to a food processor and blend until all the ingredients are combined.

2. Pour the mixture into a small dish (15–20cm in diameter) to help it freeze more quickly. You need to leave it to freeze for a minimum of 5 hours until frozen but still scoopable.

CHEESE AND SESAME SEED STRAWS

Prep: 8 minutes
Cook: 10 minutes
Makes: 12 straws

I love a cheese straw and these are super quick and easy to make, and are perfect to bring out for party occasions. The ones you buy at the shops can be quite salty, so these make ideal toddler versions that all the guests will love too. Cheese straws also make great little dipping tools for kids to dip into hummus, guacamole or purées.

320g ready-rolled puff pastry
50g mature cheddar cheese, grated
drizzle of olive oil
2 tbsp sesame seeds

1. Preheat the oven to 220°C/200°C fan. Line a baking tray with greaseproof paper.

2. Unroll the pastry sheet and lay it horizontally in front of you, keeping the greaseproof paper on the back. Sprinkle the cheddar all over the pasty sheet. Push the cheese lightly into the pastry, then drizzle with a little oil and sprinkle over the sesame seeds.

3. Using a knife, carefully cut the pastry down the middle to divide it in half, then cut 6 x 3cm thick strips on each side so you have 12 strips. Remove the pastry strips one at a time from the paper and carefully twist each 'straw', holding the top and bottom and twisting in opposite directions about 4–5 times so you get a lovely swirl shape.

4. Place the straws on the tray and keep going with the remaining pastry.

5. Bake for 8–10 minutes, or until golden and crispy. Leave to cool a little then enjoy. Store the straws in an airtight container for around 3 days to keep them nice and crispy.

Try using chia seeds or milled seeds in this recipe too for variety.

APPLE DOUGHNUT SLICES

V A ❄

Prep: 10 minutes,
          plus 1–2 hours' freezing time
Makes: 10–15 'doughnuts'

These 'doughnuts' are so fun – they look brilliant as a party spread and are nice and easy to make. They also taste great with a sweet and sour vibe. You can vary the toppings and add whatever you fancy – sprinkles, chopped fruits or even some chia seed jam (see page 122). Your toddler will love these and they can easily get involved with making them too. You'll need to let these ones defrost a bit before serving.

2–3 large apples
125ml Greek or coconut yoghurt
20g milled seeds or ground nuts
a few chunks of dark chocolate, grated
1 tbsp peanut butter, thinned down
   with 1 tbsp hot water

1. Peel and trim the tops off the apples so they are flat and remove the core. Slice the apples across into super-thin (roughly 0.5cm) slices through the middle to create 'doughnuts'. Do this until you have used up all the apples.

2. Dry the slices with kitchen roll and spread the top of each one with coconut or Greek yoghurt and then choose your topping: shake over the seeds/ground nuts, grate over the chocolate or swirl some thinned peanut butter on top.

3. Put the doughnuts onto a small tray (which will fit in the freezer). You might need to do this in a few batches.

4. Freeze for 1–2 hours until the yoghurt topping is frozen. Remove from the freezer 5–10 minutes before serving so the apple isn't too chilly and hard to bite!

MINI BLACK FOREST CHERRY CAKES

V A

Prep: 15 minutes
Cook: 15 minutes
Makes: 18 mini cakes

This is one of my favourite recipes from this book and always goes down a treat with my family; the chocolate and cherry combo is a firm winner. These cakes don't have a lot of sugar in them – just the jam, which is combined with the cherries, making them a really great option for a party or even as a snack.

200g frozen cherries, defrosted, plus a handful for decorating, finely chopped (reserve the cherry juice from the defrosted fruit for later)
2 tbsp cherry jam (or another fruit jam)
2 tbsp cocoa powder
2 tbsp boiling water
80g unsalted butter, at room temperature, or dairy-free spread
1 large free-range egg, beaten, or 1 flaxseed egg (see page 109)
50g ground almonds
100g self-raising flour
1 tsp baking powder

To decorate
100g crème fraîche or dairy-free alternative
a few chunks of dark chocolate, grated

These are great cakes to make for parties and look beautiful as a centrepiece. You can always use other fruits or swap yoghurt for crème fraîche.

1. Preheat the oven to 200°C/180°C fan. Line a mini cupcake or muffin tin with 18 cases.

2. Add most of the cherries and jam to a food processor and blitz until blended to a purée.

3. In a small bowl, mix the cocoa powder with the boiling water and stir until it forms a paste.

4. Add the butter or spread, egg and cocoa powder paste to the food processor and blitz until combined with the cherry purée. Then add the almonds, flour and baking powder and give it a pulse to mix together.

5. Divide the mixture between the cases and bake for 10–15 minutes, or until cooked through and fluffy-looking. Use a skewer to check the middle – it should come out clean.

6. Leave to cool in the tin for 5 minutes, then transfer to a cooling rack to cool completely.

7. Top with a teaspoon of crème fraîche, the reserved finely chopped cherries, a drizzle of the reserved juice and a sprinkle of dark chocolate to finish. You can store these in the fridge and enjoy for up to 2 days.

LOWER-SUGAR SPONGE CAKE

V

Prep: 10 minutes
Cook: 20–25 minutes
Makes: a single layer cake

This cake is lower in sugar than many traditional celebration cakes but still tastes great and looks amazing. You can really go to town with this, adding lots of colourful fruit on top, plus candles and cake toppers if it's for a birthday party. I think this cake is such a fab option for toddlers' parties!

150g blueberries
60g light brown sugar
90g Greek yoghurt
4 tbsp olive oil
180ml milk of choice
180g plain flour
1½ tsp baking powder
100g cream cheese, for topping
handful of fresh fruit (such as mango, strawberries and raspberries), to serve

1. Preheat the oven to 200°C/180°C fan. Grease a 20cm loose-bottomed cake tin.

2. Place 100g of the blueberries into a pan with 10g of the sugar and a splash of water. Mash it all down and let it cook for 3–4 minutes to create a sort of jammy sauce. Leave to cool.

3. Use a stand mixer or electric whisk to beat together the yoghurt, oil and the rest of the sugar until it is all combined. Stir in the milk, then mix in the flour and baking powder. Swirl through half of the jammy mixture, drop in the remaining blueberries and stir.

4. Pour the cake mix into the tin and spread it around to make it even. Bake for 20–25 minutes or until it is cooked through and golden on top.

5. Let the cake cool in the tin for 5 minutes before turning it out onto a cooling rack to cool completely.

6. Mix the cream cheese with the rest of the blueberry jam. Once the cake has cooled completely, spread it on top, top with fresh fruit and serve. This cake has a cream cheese topping, so it will need to be stored in the fridge and shouldn't be left at room temperature for more than 4 hours.

If you want to make it a layered cake, like in the picture, simply double the recipe and add a whole extra layer.

FRUIT TART
V A ❄

Prep: 15 minutes,
          plus 30 minutes' chilling in the fridge
Cook: 25–30 minutes
Makes: 12 slices

This tart looks wonderful as part of a party spread. It's quite a special option and is super versatile, as you can really mix and match the toppings and add your little one's favourite fruits. It's quite a rich option, so you really don't need much per serving.

- -

plain flour, for dusting
320g block of shortcrust pastry
250g mascarpone cheese
225ml double cream
150g Greek yoghurt
250g fresh fruit (kiwi, satsumas or
    berries, such as strawberries,
    raspberries or blueberries work well)

1. Roll out the pastry on a lightly dusted surface to approximately 1cm thick. Push the pastry into the edges of a 23cm fluted tart tin, leaving the pastry overhanging (you will trim this later).

2. Prick the pastry base with a fork and chill for about 30 minutes in the fridge.

3. Preheat the oven to 200°C/180°C fan.

4. Remove the pastry base from the fridge and line with a scrunched-up piece of greaseproof paper. Pour over some baking beans (raw beans, pulses or rice will do if you don't have any) and place onto a baking tray, then into the oven and bake for 15 minutes. Remove the beans and paper and bake for a further 10–15 minutes, or until the pastry is lovely and golden (it will not need any more baking now).

5. Remove from the oven and leave to cool completely in the tin. Once fully cooled, trim the edges using a peeler so that the offcuts are shaved off and the edges are all even. Dust off any crumbs and leave to be filled (the baked pastry base can be wrapped and stored in an airtight container for 3 days).

6. To make the filling, whisk the mascarpone and cream until they are combined and hold gentle peaks. Mix in the Greek yoghurt. Pour the mixture into the baked case and smooth over a little.

7. Decorate with the fresh fruit however you fancy and then cut into slices. You can store this tart in the fridge for up to 2 days.

 Experiment with the toppings by using your little one's favourite fruits or writing their name or age on top in colourful fruits.

SALAD KEBABS

Prep: 8 minutes
Makes: 12 kebabs

These are a fun way to get toddlers enjoying their veggies and fruits – they look great and are really easy to make too. Older children can help you make these, but be careful with the skewers with younger toddlers – you can always make the skewers blunt once you've popped the fruit and veggies on! These are great for a BBQ or birthday party for all the guests.

For the kebabs
¼ cucumber (about 130g)
1 large apple, peeled, cored and cut into very thin slices
50g little gem lettuce, trimmed and leaves snapped off
150g cantaloupe melon, peeled, deseeded and sliced into thin wedges
12 cherry tomatoes, quartered
125g cheese, cut into thin slices (optional)

For the dressing
1 ripe avocado, destoned and skin removed
2 tbsp coconut yoghurt or cashew nut butter
1 tbsp olive oil
juice of ½ lemon

1. Start by making the dressing. Put the avocado, coconut yoghurt (or cashew nut butter), oil and lemon juice into a high-speed blender. Blitz until it creates a green avo dressing, then loosen with 25–30ml of cold water and blitz again so it's a good consistency for pouring (or keep it thicker for dipping).

2. Skewer up the fruit and veg, alternating the colours so it looks beautiful.

3. Lay the kebabs onto a platter or board and drizzle with the dressing (or leave it to one side in a jug for guests to help themselves). If you are keeping it thicker for dipping, pop it into a dish for people to dunk as they wish! This dressing makes an easy and nutrient-rich salad dressing for lots of other recipes too, and will keep in the fridge for 2 days.

 Vary what you pop onto the skewers – you can experiment hugely with fruits and veggies. Just remember to cut, slice or squash to appropriate textures for your toddler's age and abilities.

COURGETTE CORNBREAD SQUARES

Prep: 10–15 minutes
Cook: 25–30 minutes
Makes: 20–25 squares

This is one of my favourite recipes from the book – it's so tasty and makes a great snack, lunch or side, as well as being fab topped with a dollop of cream cheese and some dill or a spoonful of hummus with some ground pistachios. I love this one on its own, though, and it's now a regular in our freezer. This recipe makes a good amount and packs lots of flavours and textures. I hope your little ones will love it.

50g unsalted butter or dairy-free spread
4 spring onions, trimmed and finely chopped
2 courgettes (about 350g), trimmed and coarsely grated
1 large free-range egg, beaten
125ml milk of choice
125g Greek yoghurt
198g tin sweetcorn, drained
100g plain flour
150g cornmeal or polenta
30g mature cheddar cheese, grated

1. Preheat the oven to 200°C/180°C fan. Line a 20 x 30cm tin with greaseproof paper.

2. Melt the butter or spread in a large frying pan, add the spring onions and courgettes and cook for 10 minutes, stirring occasionally until soft and cooked down. Leave to one side to cool completely.

3. Mix the egg, milk, yoghurt and sweetcorn together in a bowl.

4. Add the flour, cornmeal, cheddar and cooled veg, and give it a good mix to combine.

5. Pour the mixture into the tin and bake for 25 minutes, or until golden and cooked through.

6. Cool in the tin then transfer to a cooling rack and cut into 20–25 squares. These will keep in an airtight container for 2 days or can be added to your freezer stash.

 Adding toppings to bread and tray bakes helps to add extra nutrients. You can also use dairy-free alternatives to replace the cheese and yoghurt.

Snacks

Many of my favourite recipes from the book are within this little section. Snacks can be a great way to help top up toddler intakes in between meals and here I have tried to provide a variety of tasty and simple options for your family.

Many of these can be batch-made and then offered throughout the week. That's something I've been doing a lot while creating these options. The veggie flapjacks are an absolute favourite with my kids and me! These snacks can easily be added to or offered in larger portions to make tasty lunches, celebration foods and even breakfasts options. Enjoy!

CARROT CAKE MUFFINS

V A ❄

Prep: 10–15 minutes
Cook: 10–15 minutes
Makes: 24 mini muffins

I'm carrying on the tradition of my 'carrot cake' range here and making it into muffins – what's not to love?! These muffins have no added sugars other than the natural sweetness of the raisins and dates, so they aren't overly sweet. If you are concerned about using whole raisins, just blend them up with the dates. This recipe is perfect to make with your toddler!

125g dates, stones removed
3 tbsp boiling water
100ml sunflower oil
2 tbsp raisins
2 large free-range eggs, beaten, or
   2 chia seed eggs (see page 109)
250g finely grated carrot
125g self-raising flour
50g walnuts, finely ground

1. Preheat the oven to 200°C/180°C fan. Line a mini cupcake or muffin tray with cases.

2. Place the dates into a small bowl with the boiling water. Leave to one side.

3. Meanwhile, mix the oil, raisins and eggs in a bowl.

4. Put the dates in a blender with the water, whizz to form a paste and stir into the raisin mixture along with the carrot. Add the flour and walnuts and stir to combine.

5. Divide the batter between the cases and bake for 10–15 minutes, or until a skewer inserted into a cupcake comes out clean.

6. Leave to cool a little in the tray, then remove to a cooling rack to cool completely. Store these in an airtight container for 3 days or freeze for up to 3 months. Once defrosted, they will be ready to eat.

SUPER-SPEEDY CARROT FRITTERS

Prep: 5 minutes
Cook: 5 minutes
Makes: 5–6 fritters

I've made fritters before and they've always gone down brilliantly with my audience, so I loved creating a different version of them for this book! The fritters can be made ahead and stored in the fridge or freezer and eaten cold or heated all the way through and served warm – whatever works! This is also a slightly less messy snack that's good for eating when out and about!

1 medium carrot (about 50g), peeled and finely grated
50g frozen sweetcorn
2 tbsp self-raising flour
1 large free-range egg, beaten, or 1 chia seed egg (see page 109)
1 tbsp olive oil
5g Parmesan cheese or dairy-free alternative, finely grated (optional)

1. Add the carrot, sweetcorn, flour and egg to a large bowl and stir to combine. Form into 5 or 6 balls and flatten out.

2. Heat the oil in a large non-stick frying pan over a medium heat. Place the flattened balls in the pan and fry for 2 minutes on each side until golden and cooked through.

3. Remove from the pan and leave to cool a little on some kitchen paper to drain any excess oil, then serve with a little Parmesan cheese sprinkled on top (if using). Any leftover fritters can be stored in the fridge for 2 days or frozen for 3 months for a quick lunch or a snack another day! They can be defrosted and eaten cold or reheated straight from frozen until piping hot.

If you freeze these, place a piece of baking paper between each fritter to stop them sticking together.

VEG-PACKED FLAPJACKS

Prep: 10–15 minutes
Cook: 20 minutes
Makes: 16 squares

These are such a colourful and easy option for a toddler's snack! We've always been a fan of the savoury flapjack, but this one is on another level! Another perfect one for making with the kids – Raffy loves cooking these with me.

100g unsalted butter or dairy-free spread
2 spring onions, trimmed and finely sliced
1 medium carrot, washed and grated
1 courgette, trimmed and grated
200g porridge oats
80g mature cheddar cheese
2 flaxseed eggs (see page 109) or 2 large free-range eggs, beaten
1 raw beetroot, peeled and grated

1. Preheat the oven to 200°C/180°C fan. Line a 20cm square ovenproof tin with greaseproof paper.

2. Melt the butter or spread in a saucepan. Add the spring onions, carrot and courgette and cook for 5 minutes, stirring occasionally.

3. Turn the heat off, stir in the oats, cheese and eggs, then fold in the beetroot (to stop the colour bleeding into it all too much).

4. Pour the mixture into the tin and press down to make it all even on top. Bake for 20 minutes, or until golden and cooked through. Leave to cool in the tin completely, then cut into 16 squares before serving. Store these in an airtight container for 3 days or add any leftovers to your freezer stash. Once defrosted, they are ready to eat.

Grating veggies into dinners, snacks and even puddings is a great way to add colour, vibrancy and some extra nutrients.

CHOCOLATE RAISIN BREAD

Prep: 10 minutes
Cook: 30 minutes
Makes: 1 loaf

This was one of the first recipes I wanted to create for this book and I did a lot of experimentation with it! Raffy loves a fruit bread and this is a great alternative – it's a bit like a malt loaf but with a little hit from the sweet banana flavour. Raffy calls it 'chocolate raisin bread', hence the title of the recipe! This is neither sweet nor savoury and doesn't have a super-chocolatey flavour, but it really hits the spot and looks fab for little ones. For younger toddlers, soak the raisins for a few minutes or chop them up super small.

3 large ripe bananas, peeled
75ml vegetable oil
4 tbsp milk of choice
225g self-raising flour
2 tbsp cocoa powder
1 tsp mixed spice
100g raisins, soaked or well chopped

1. Preheat the oven to 200°C/180°C fan. Line a 900g loaf tin with greaseproof paper.

2. Mash the bananas in a bowl, then add the oil and milk and stir together.

3. Add the flour, cocoa powder and mixed spice and mix well. Stir in the raisins.

4. Pour the batter into the tin and bake for 30 minutes, or until browned on top and cooked through, so a skewer inserted into the centre of the loaf comes out clean. Leave to cool a little in the tin (it will firm up as it cools) before slicing and serving. You can store this bread in an airtight container for 3 days or freeze for another day.

 You can add toppings like chopped fruit or a little jam to this, but we enjoy it with just a little spread of butter.

MIXED SEED CRACKER

V ⅄ ❄

Prep: 10 minutes
Cook: 12–15 minutes
Makes: 35–40 crackers

- - - - - - - - - -

300g wholemeal or plain flour, plus
   extra for dusting
½ tsp baking powder
1 tbsp milled seeds
2 tbsp poppy seeds
½ tbsp fennel seeds, ground (optional)
30g unsalted butter, cold from the
   fridge, or dairy-free spread

> Try adding some ground ginger, cumin
> or paprika to the recipe, which really
> make the crackers pop!

I'm always asked about 'crackers' for toddlers as parents are often worried about the salt content. Therefore, I wanted to come up with a non-crumbly cracker without the extra salt, and I think this recipe really hits the spot. It's a very plain cracker, but that makes it even better for adding spreads to, for dipping or (as Ada loves it) just eating it plain.

1. Preheat the oven to 200°C/180°C fan. Line two large baking trays with greaseproof paper.

2. Mix the flour, baking powder, milled seeds, poppy seeds and fennel seeds (if using) in a bowl. Rub in the butter or spread, then add some cold water gradually – approximately 175ml should be enough – stirring to combine until you have a dough. Once it is nearly combined, pop the dough onto a flour-dusted surface and knead it for 5 minutes until it is smooth.

3. Using a rolling pin, roll out the dough until it is 0.5cm thick. Now you can either cut it into squares, use a 6cm cutter to make rounds or just freestyle it. Cut into shapes until you get about 35–40 crackers. (You can reroll the offcuts until you cannot make any more.) Transfer the crackers to the trays.

4. Prick the crackers with a fork and bake for 12–15 minutes, or until golden and fairly hard. Leave to cool a little on the trays, then remove to a cooling rack to cool completely before eating. These crackers will keep well in an airtight container for around 3 days. If you don't need a big batch, cut the dough in half at step 2 and freeze. When you're ready, defrost the dough and continue to step 3.

AVOCADO ICE LOLLY

Prep: 5 minutes,
        plus 4–5 hours' freezing time
Makes: 6–8 lollies,
        depending on the lolly mould size

This fab recipe is totally different to your standard ice cream! Both my two love these lollies and they contain some healthy fats and nutrients too. It's super easy to make the recipe dairy-free by using coconut yoghurt and dairy-free milk. It is a lovely combo and a great way to give toddlers a little something that feels more exciting than your average snack!

. . . .

1 large ripe avocado, stoned and
  peeled
1 ripe banana, peeled
4 tbsp apple juice (or water)
grated zest of 1 lime and juice of ½
150g Greek yoghurt or
  coconut yoghurt
100ml milk of choice
1–2 tbsp milled seeds and nuts
  (optional), to serve

1. Roughly cut up the avocado flesh and banana and add to a blender along with the apple juice (or water) and lime zest and juice. Blend until smooth, then add the yoghurt and whizz again until it is all combined.

2. Add the milk and whizz again.

3. Pour the mixture into the lolly moulds and freeze for 4–5 hours, or until fully frozen.

4. Serve as they are or dunk them into a little extra yoghurt and the milled seeds and nuts.

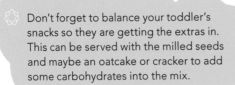

Don't forget to balance your toddler's snacks so they are getting the extras in. This can be served with the milled seeds and maybe an oatcake or cracker to add some carbohydrates into the mix.

GARLIC AND OREGANO STICKS

V A ❄

Prep: 10 minutes
Cook: 7 minutes
Makes: 16 sticks

This toddler-friendly version of garlic bread is so fab as a snack and is lovely to have on the side of lunch or dinner. The sticks can be served with soups or stews or with some sticks of veggies and a dip.

270g (½ large loaf) ciabatta
1 garlic clove, peeled
1 tbsp dried oregano
40g unsalted butter, at room temperature, or dairy-free spread

1. Preheat the oven to 220°C/200°C fan. Line a baking tray with greaseproof paper.

2. Cut the ciabatta in half widthways, then cut each half into 4 strips lengthways. Then cut each strip in half. You should now have 8 smaller lengths. Repeat this with the second half of ciabatta so you have 16 sticks.

3. To make the garlic butter, use a pestle and mortar to bash the garlic and oregano into a paste, then mix into the softened butter or spread. Alternatively, place the butter or spread into a bowl, stir in the oregano and then finely grate in the garlic and mash together.

4. Spread the garlic butter on one side of the ciabatta sticks and place on the tray. Bake for 7 minutes, turning for the last 2 minutes, or until golden and smelling delicious. You can freeze these after step 3, prior to baking, and you can bake them straight from frozen.

GREEN DIP

Having a fab go-to dip recipe is always handy, and this one can also be used as a pasta sauce – just add a tablespoon to some cooked pasta, grate over some cheese, and lunch or dinner is sorted!

Prep: 5 minutes
Makes: 400g

. . . .

50g broccoli, cut into small florets
25g spinach, washed
½ ripe avocado, stoned and peeled
400g tin chickpeas (in water)
good pinch of ground cumin
good squeeze of lemon juice

1. In a blender, add the broccoli, spinach, avocado, chickpeas (and chickpea water) and cumin, and blend to a smooth, thick paste. Squeeze in the lemon juice.

2. Serve with toast soldiers, pitta bread or the crackers from page 190.

 This dip can be stored in the fridge for 2 days or frozen for up to 3 months.

RASPBERRY DROPS WITH YOGHURT

Prep: 5 minutes
Cook: 4–6minutes
Makes: 14 drops

These fast became Raffy's favourite when I was testing the recipes for this book. They have some sweetness from the banana but also lots of bitter notes from the raspberries and come packed with nutrients from all the seeds. And the best thing? They are super quick to whizz together and can be batch-cooked and frozen for later!

1 ripe banana, peeled
80g raspberries
25ml milk of choice
35g self-raising flour
1 tsp ground cinnamon
2 tsp chia seeds
1 tbsp milled seeds
drizzle of olive oil
50g yoghurt or dairy-free alternative
    per person, to serve

1. Mash the banana and raspberries into a bowl, adding the milk to combine.

2. Add the flour, cinnamon, chia seeds and milled seeds, and give it another good mix.

3. Heat the oil in a medium frying pan over a medium heat. Add half a tablespoon (a 'drop') of the mixture into the pan until you have about 14 (you will need to do in batches, maybe 8 at a time), and cook for 2–3 minutes on each side, or until golden and cooked through.

4. Leave to cool then serve with a little pot of yoghurt for dunking. (When warm they are nice and gooey, but will go more solid as they cool.) Store these in the fridge for 2 days or freeze. Defrost overnight in the fridge, or for a couple of hours in a lunch box, and they will be ready to eat!

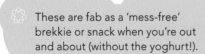

These are fab as a 'mess-free' brekkie or snack when you're out and about (without the yoghurt!).

TOMATO SCONES

Prep: 15 minutes
Cook: 10–15 minutes
Makes: 16–18 scones

Raffy has always been a big fan of scones, but when buying them or eating them from cafés they often contain a large amount of salt and sugar, which is fine on occasion, but I wanted to make some delicious scones that were lower in salt but still packed plenty of flavour. These scones are such a winner for an out-and-about snack. I love having a stash of these in the freezer or an airtight container for the kids (and me!). They are so simple to make and I often get the kids to help me out.

300g self-raising flour, plus extra
  for dusting
150g cheddar cheese, grated
250g Greek yoghurt
150g on-the-vine cherry tomatoes,
  finely chopped
1 tsp smoked sweet paprika
4 black olives, stoned, finely chopped
  (optional)

1. Preheat the oven to 200°C/180°C fan. Line two baking trays with greaseproof paper.

2. In a bowl, combine the flour, 130g of the cheese, and the yoghurt, tomatoes, paprika and olives (if using).

3. Use your hands to form the mixture into a ball, then pop it onto a flour-dusted surface, adding a little more flour if it gets too sticky to work with. Knead the dough with your hands for a few minutes until it feels a little smoother.

4. Roll out the dough to 2cm thick. Using a 5cm cutter, cut out 16–18 scones. (You can reroll the offcuts until you can't make any more.)

5. Grate or sprinkle the remaining cheese on top of each scone.

6. Bake for 10–15 minutes, or until cooked through. Leave to cool a little before serving. You can store these in an airtight container for a few days or freeze to enjoy at a later date!

TROUBLE- SHOOTING TIPS

5

Troubleshooting Tips

When it comes to feeding toddlers, I know that there are so many burning questions that parents have. I've tried to include the most common questions that I'm asked around feeding toddlers in this chapter so you can get some quickfire answers, right now.

Should we limit how much fruit our toddler has?

Not necessarily! Fruit is a great food with lots of nutrients and fibre, and it also provides hydrating fluid. However, many children will often choose fruit and refuse veg and/or other foods. Ideally we want to see a nice balance, so try to keep offering more savoury options and plenty of veggies too. If some days your toddler has lots of fruit, think about altering the balance the next day and offering more in the way of veggies. It might take a while, but remember it's familiarisation that leads to acceptance (see page 30).

My toddler will only eat food with their hands... help!

This is often about children wanting to have some control over mealtimes. It's OK to let them get a little messy at mealtimes, so using their hands to self-feed is fine. Try not to draw too much attention to it and keep gently encouraging them to try the cutlery by loading it for them. Also do lots of role modelling and offer subtle praise when they use their cutlery well: for example, 'Good work with that spoon'.

My toddler is eating huge portions… is this OK?

Children are pretty good at regulating their own appetites, especially in the early years. So try not to worry too much about this and follow the advice 'you decide what to offer and let them decide how much' (see page 34). If you're worried at all, I'd recommend visiting your GP or health visitor and getting your little one's weight and height monitored fairly regularly, mainly for your own peace of mind.

I've tried all the strategies and my toddler still won't eat many foods. What can I do?

This question is hard to answer without details, but a good registered nutritionist or dietitian should be able to support you with getting to the bottom of the food refusal, so see if you can seek out some support. Otherwise, one thing to really try is consistency. It's so easy to put some of these skills into place and try for a short while before giving in or reverting to old habits. However, when it comes to food refusal, consistency really is so key!

My toddler has started throwing food/cutlery – help!

This is a common thing that can make mealtimes a bit fraught. Sometimes kids are just experimenting when they throw food, and a bit of that is OK. But if it becomes a regular occurrence it can be tricky. This is what has been working for me:

- Not drawing too much attention to the throwing.
- Responding calmly and in the same way each time.
- Using a phrase such as 'That's not what we do with food – if you don't want it put it on the table', each time it happens.
- Introducing a side plate for them to add 'unwanted' foods to and role model using it yourself.
- Offering subtle and specific praise when they do this and it's not thrown, e.g., 'Well done for using your side plate'.
- Being really consistent with the response each time.

Can I offer my toddler herbs and spices in their meals?

Herbs and spices can be introduced right from the start of your child's journey with food! It's so good to experiment with them as they then get used to a whole range of new flavours. Try to use the ones you use in your own cooking as much as possible. Start small and build up gradually. It's also OK to offer some 'plainer' foods too, so your little one doesn't always have to have foods flavoured in order to eat them.

My toddler has a cow's milk protein allergy (CPMA). What are good calcium sources to offer them?

Non-dairy sources of calcium are increasingly easy to find and include:

- fortified plant milks
- tinned fish with soft bones (e.g. sardines)
- beans and lentils
- nuts and seeds (ground or nut butters)
- dark-green leafy veggies
- calcium-set tofu
- brown bread

When can I offer my toddler crunchy things like raw carrot and apple?

This will vary from child to child depending on how well developed their oral motor skills are. However, raw carrot and raw apple can be a choking hazard, so they are not ideal. You can always cook these foods or grate or thinly slice them and offer them raw for younger toddlers (see page 85). At around four or five years these foods might be something your toddler is able to cope with better as their oral motor skills develop.

Should I avoid giving my toddler protein at dinnertime?

This is a myth. It's absolutely fine to offer your little one protein in the evening – it won't stop them sleeping. Babies often have milk before bed, which is a protein-rich food. Just make sure you leave enough time after dinner – perhaps an hour or so – for them to go to bed without a full tummy.

My toddler is unwell and they have now gone off their food. How can I get them back on track with their eating?

It's so normal for children to go off their food when they are unwell and, even after they are better, they might still not have their normal appetite back. When this happens, try to stay calm and keep those mealtimes pressure-free as much as possible. Keep to a similar structure of meal timings and continue to offer variety, while also offering a few extras that they are more likely to want to eat, for example, milk, yoghurt or fruit. Speak to your GP if you're worried.

I feel like I've failed – my toddler will only eat five safe foods!

You certainly haven't failed! Feeding kids can be tough, but it's never too late to put positive practices into place. Branching out from safe foods can seem daunting, but it's about building their confidence and familiarity with new foods. Think about ways you can 'expose' your child to other foods without them eating it (see page 30) and try to offer any new foods:

- in small amounts
- along with a safe food or two
- without any pressure to eat it

Help – my toddler will only eat in front of the TV!

This can be really common with parents who have been struggling with food refusal. It can seem easier to offer toddlers TV as a distraction, which often gets them to eat. However, this is often a short-term win and, actually, eating with distractions isn't great for helping little ones to enjoy foods in the long run. Ideally, try to have separate times for play or TV and keep mealtimes about the food and eating, as much as you can. You might need to:

- Explain you won't be watching TV at mealtimes anymore or gradually reduce the occurrence of TV meals.

- Have a schedule for food time and TV/play time and stick to it.

- Get your toddler involved in choosing the menu – you could give them two options or offer foods you know they will eat.

- Keep mealtimes light and pressure-free, and engage your little one in things they are interested in at mealtimes if you can.

THANK YOUS

I've loved writing this book. It really was such a collaborative piece and there are so many people to thank! Firstly, I must thank my family – my husband Danny and my kids, Raffy and Adaline, for the time that writing this has taken away from you, but also for being so involved. Being chief recipe testers for me on a daily basis and even coming along to a long photoshoot to get the cover and the family shots in the book. Raffy and Adaline, you were both brilliant and absolute professionals in front of the camera. None of this would have happened without you all. Thank you.

A big shout out to all the people who worked on the book too – to everyone at Bev James Management, especially Morwenna, for supporting me to get here in the first place. Also to everyone at Penguin – Sam Jackson, Leah Feltham and Marta Catalano for all your work on the books. I know it was tricky project. Julia and Emma were excellent editors too and I'm so grateful for how well you managed to condense my words and meanings. The food styling and the food photography were INCREDIBLE, as ever – thank you to Liz & Max and Frankie and Sara. Thank you to Christina Mackenzie and Bee Berrie for all your support with testing these brilliant recipes for me, too. A huge thank you to ALL the experts who mentored, reviewed and supported me with the writing of this book: Marion Heatherington, Emma Haycraft, Dr Anna Colton, Sigrid Gibson, Giles Yeo, Catherine Lippe, Laura Matthews, Claire Baseley, Stacey Zimmels and Jenna Brown. I also want to thank my friends who brought their little toddler models to the shoot. I'm SO grateful to you guys – Anna, Olivia and Amy. Thank you to Sophie Rogers too, for your amazing support!

Lastly, I want to say a HUGE thank you to those of you who read my blog each week, who follow me and support me on social media. Without your support, encouragement and BRILLIANT questions every day I don't think I could have possibly written *How to Feed Your Toddler*. THANK YOU for making this happen.

Charlotte xXx

1

Vermilion, an imprint of Ebury Publishing,
20 Vauxhall Bridge Road,
London SW1V 2SA

Vermilion is part of the Penguin Random House group of companies whose addresses can be found at global.penguinrandomhouse.com

Penguin
Random House
UK

Copyright © Charlotte Stirling-Reed 2022
Photography © Haarala Hamilton 2022
Illustrations © Lucie Stericker, Studio 7:15 2022

Charlotte Stirling-Reed has asserted her right to be identified as the author of this Work in accordance with the Copyright, Designs and Patents Act 1988

First published by Vermilion in 2022

www.penguin.co.uk

A CIP catalogue record for this book is available from the British Library

Commissioning Editor: Sam Jackson
Project Editors: Marta Catalano, Leah Feltham, Julia Kellaway
Editors: Julia Kellaway, Emma Bastow
Designer: Lucie Stericker, Studio 7:15
Photographer: Haarala Hamilton
Food & Prop Stylist: Frankie Unsworth
Food safety guidance: Jenna Brown

ISBN 9781785044052

Printed and bound in Italy by L.E.G.O S.p.A.

The authorised representative in the EEA is Penguin Random House Ireland, Morrison Chambers, 32 Nassau Street, Dublin D02 YH68.

Penguin Random House is committed to a sustainable future for our business, our readers and our planet. This book is made from Forest Stewardship Council® certified paper.

The information in this book has been compiled as general guidance on the specific subjects addressed. It is not a substitute and not to be relied on for medical, healthcare or pharmaceutical professional advice. Please consult your GP before changing, stopping or starting any medical treatment. So far as the author is aware the information given is correct and up to date as at May 2022. Practice, laws and regulations all change and the reader should obtain up-to-date professional advice on any such issues. The author and publishers disclaim, as far as the law allows, any liability arising directly or indirectly from the use or misuse of the information contained in this book.